SUPER*fast*
F O O D S

Also by Michael Van Straten and Barbara Griggs,
published by Dorling Kindersley
Superfoods
The Superfoods Diet Book

SUPER*fast*
FOODS

MICHAEL VAN STRATEN
AND
BARBARA GRIGGS

DORLING KINDERSLEY
LONDON · NEW YORK · STUTTGART

A DORLING KINDERSLEY BOOK

Editor: Mark Ronan
Art Editor: Phil Kay
Managing Editor: Krystyna Mayer
Managing Art Editor: Derek Coombes
DTP Designer: Doug Miller
Production Controller: Stephen Stuart
Illustrations: Madeleine David

First published in Great Britain in 1994
by Dorling Kindersley Limited
9 Henrietta Street, London WC2E 8PS

Reprinted 1994

A CIP catalogue record for this book is available from the British Library

ISBN 0 7513 0088 8

Reproduced by IGS, Radstock, Avon
Printed and bound by Bath Press, Avon

CONTENTS

ACKNOWLEDGMENTS

The authors would like to thank the following authors and publishers for their permission to quote excerpts from their work:

Marcella Hazan *The Essentials of Classic Italian Cooking* (Macmillan London Ltd.); Pat Chapman *Favourite Restaurant Curries* (Judy Piatkus Publishers Ltd.); *The New School Cookbook* (privately published by The New School, Rome); and Marlene Nijhof for permission to quote two of her recipes.

They would also like to thank J. Sainsbury plc for permission to reproduce a recipe from one of their leaflets; Oona van den Berg, who created a number of delicious recipes specially for the book; Presia Eyles, for very kindly sharing a number of her favourite Superfast Food recipes; Margery Brooks, who tested – and often improved – many recipes for us, and contributed some of her own; Sally Pearce; Henri van der Zee; Shirley Dineen; Felicity Green; and other kind friends for their recipes, suggestions, and encouragement.

A special thank you to Janet Betley for assembling, ordering, and collating the recipe section; and to Mark Ronan, our patient and indefatigable editor at Dorling Kindersley.

MESSAGE FROM THE AUTHORS

This is the age of speed. Everyone today lives life at the double, and people seem to have less and less time to spare. There are more and more single-parent families. There are more and more working wives and mothers struggling to combine a full-time job with running a home and raising children, and more and more single, young working men and women whose high-speed lifestyles don't allow for leisurely hours in the kitchen. As a result, the nostalgic picture of the family sitting around the dinner table together to enjoy good home cooking is fading fast. Many of today's teenagers no longer know what regular mealtimes are. Instead, they "graze" as the mood takes them.

The universal cry from everyone required to cook, whether for themselves, for their family, or for their friends, is that there is never enough time. This is the reason for the phenomenal growth in recent years in the sale and profits of take-away food from burger bars, fast-food restaurants, chip shops, pie shops, and supermarkets. And this is why we have written *Superfast Foods* – to show how easy it is to make meals that are delicious and nourishing without spending lots of time and lots of money.

Michael van Straten

Barbara Griggs

INTRODUCTION

Superfast Foods is a more than just a cookery book. It is a cookery book that is also about eating healthily – even when you're pushed for time. You will find all you need to know about healthy eating and nutrition summarized in the first four chapters, without the tedious statistics and percentages that make the debate confusing. Because different sectors of the population have distinct nutritional needs – over and above broad, general guidelines – we have sketched out profiles based on nine different population groups. Find the one you identify with most closely, and follow the suggestions for specific nutrients of which you may be especially in need. Each of these case studies includes short lists of the Superfoods that could be particularly good sources of these nutrients, and suggestions for a week's choice of recipes for the main meal, plus ideas for the extras that will turn it into a complete, well-balanced meal.

The A–Z of Superfoods *(see pages 167–173)* is a glossary of foods – including herbs and spices – that are especially recommended for their nutritional value. The profiles of each Superfood include information on their individual components that can affect our health and vitality.

In the recipe section you will find almost 200 recipes for simple, delicious dishes that can form the basis of a nourishing, well-balanced meal. There are dishes that take only a few minutes to prepare and a few minutes to cook. There are also dishes that may take 10 or 15 minutes to prepare, but can then be left to cook or marinate for some time, while you get on with something else. These include stews, casseroles, and marinated dishes. The recipes include dishes that will be enjoyed by everyone – children and teenagers, students and young single people, wives and mothers trying to be Superwoman, busy families, and people living on their own, who may be disinclined to spend ages preparing their meals.

Recipes for starters have been avoided on the principle that when you're in a rush to get a decent meal together, you're certainly not going to bother with complex hors-d'œuvres and delicate consommés. We have included plenty of substantial soups, however *(see pages 78–83)*, which can become meals in themselves, with the addition of a wholemeal roll, a salad, and a piece of fruit.

By the same token, there are few puddings. An apple, a peach, or a bunch of grapes is perfect for rounding off a Superfast Foods meal – all the preparation it needs is a thorough rinse. For more festive occasions, though, a few desserts have been included *(see pages 156–160)*. More than just sweet treats, they're also packed with goodness.

When you're in a hurry, the greens often get omitted from the menu altogether because they seem too much trouble. Furthermore, many children and teenagers find them so boring that they never eat them. So there are plenty of suggestions for making everyday vegetables just that little bit different and more interesting, without requiring too much time to prepare *(see pages 125–135)*.

Inviting friends to share a meal with you is one of the oldest and most precious of all human customs. Don't neglect it simply because you feel you don't have the time, or can't cope with the extra effort involved. In the Menus *(see pages 165–166)*, you will find suggestions for a selection of seasonal menus for entertaining, which will delight your friends without leaving you too limp to enjoy yourself. If you have little time for cooking, you probably don't have much time either to plan meals. With this in mind, you can consult the Last-minute Menus, devised for occasions when you will have to organize a square meal in minutes. On these occasions, you will also find the advice in The Superfast Food Kitchen *(see pages 27–33)*, on maintaining a well-stocked and well-equipped Superfast Foods kitchen, indispensable.

THE FAST-FOOD REVOLUTION

Fast food can be good food. Fast food can be as delicious as any gourmet meal produced by a couple of hours' toil in the kitchen, and it can be as nutritious as the exotic meals on offer in the priciest health farm. If you choose Superfast Foods, you'll enjoy a diet rich not only in the most important ingredient – enjoyability – but also in the vital nutrients that you need to keep healthy and full of beans.

Fast food, however, has earned itself a bad name. We feel guilty when we open a tin or a packet of frozen vegetables, or dish up baked beans on toast, instead of a properly cooked dinner. Indeed, for millions of people fast food is a nutritional disaster. At its worst, fast food is high in fats, sugar, salt, additives, and calories, and low in vitamins, minerals, and fibre. In the relentless search for the minimum effort and time spent in the kitchen, the public are paying a high price for convenience – a high price in terms of nutritional value for money, and a high price in terms of health.

What is particularly disturbing is the enormous influence that children exert on family shopping trends – and consequently on family eating habits. A recent survey conducted by a British supermarket chain showed that 48 per cent of children strongly influence their parents' choice of food. And what do children urge their mothers to buy? A third of all chocolate sold annually in Great Britain, 40 per cent of pizzas sold annually, 35 per cent of hamburgers, and 35 per cent of chips. Few children grow up enjoying fresh fruit and vegetables: only 6 per cent of spending on these was influenced by children. In the light of the most recent studies, this doesn't come as a surprise. In the survey, 19 per cent of the children were shown to be fussy, demanding eaters, who insist on having their own favourite foods – crisps, chocolate, ice cream, biscuits, and chips – rather than joining the grown-ups for a "proper" meal. Surveys of what children and teenagers eat are profoundly depressing. In 1986, the British government finally released details of the biggest postwar survey of the kind of food youngsters are eating in Britain today. It showed that chips, crisps, cakes, and biscuits featured heavily in the diets of almost all the children surveyed; that fat intake was much too high; and that four out of five children were not eating the kind of food that makes up a healthy diet. If you think these are just scaremongering statistics, the following is what one of Britain's most respected food experts, Professor Philip James, had to say about the survey's findings: "This type of diet is precisely what one would expect from a country with the highest risk of heart disease in the world, and clearly the type of food they are getting at school is even worse than the food they're getting at home." A recent survey of over 500 Australian schoolchildren aged eight to 14, from a wide range of economic backgrounds, carried out at Heidelberg in Victoria, makes just as gloomy reading – 15 per cent of the children were overweight, while a further 15 per cent were actually obese. The United States dietary recommendation about fat suggests that no more than 30 per cent of total calorie intake should come from fats. For the schoolboys in the Australian survey, however, the average fat intake ranged from 36 to 50 per cent, while for the girls it went from 36 per cent to a horrific 88 per cent.

There's a general belief that nobody in the affluent West suffers from serious nutritional deficiencies. This is a comforting theory. However, further surveys conducted in the United States, Canada, Australia, and Great Britain, have focused on what is missing in unbalanced diets. Among vital nutrients especially likely to be low are vitamins A, C, E, and the B-complex, the minerals iron, zinc, calcium, and magnesium, and fibre. In practice, specialists in nutrition-related disease are seeing huge numbers of people who have subclinical deficiencies. This means that they may be getting enough vitamin C to prevent scurvy, enough vitamin D to avoid the horrors of rickets, and enough iron to save them from severe anaemia. There is a substantial difference, however, between the minimum intake of essential nutrients necessary to keep you alive, and the level which will give you health and vitality. Heart disease and cancer are not the only two diseases closely related to poor diet – although these are the two that hit the headlines because they kill. Many other disabling illnesses are closely linked to an inadequate diet. Tiredness takes more people to their doctors than any other problem, and is near-universal among today's teenagers. It can be caused by low iron or vitamin B1 intake, and by the seesawing of blood sugar levels that result from erratic eating habits. Osteoporosis may be triggered by the menopause, but it is also the accumulative result of a low intake of calcium and other vital minerals. Many forms of cancer are closely linked with a low consumption of foods containing the antioxidant vitamins A, C, and E. Obesity, often the trigger of fatigue, back pain, arthritis, high blood pressure, raised cholesterol, and heart disease, is almost exclusively the result of poor eating habits, and is increasingly common today in both children and adults. The monumental 1991 Health Survey for England found that in just the five years previous to the survey, the proportion of obese men aged 16 to 64 had nearly doubled from 7 per cent to 13 per cent, while the proportion of obese women had increased from 12 per cent to 15 per cent. The survey also found that rather more than this number – 16 per cent of men and 17 per cent of women – had high blood pressure. Digestive and bowel disorders, skin problems, hair loss, depression, and fertility problems are also among the growing list of diseases that are linked with the junk-food diets that are increasingly replacing real food in the West today.

Family eating habits are changing for the worse. In more and more families, good, sit-down meals hardly ever happen. There is evidence that many children never actually sit down at the table for a family meal. Instead, they help themselves from the fridge, or load a fast snack, such as hamburgers, pizzas, and oven chips, into the microwave oven. Hard-working mothers, living on the wrong kind of convenience foods and ready-made snacks, are too tired even to think about planning meals, let alone spend time in the kitchen preparing them. This becomes a vicious circle: poor food, more exhaustion, less energy, even worse food. Tired mothers, of course, don't have the energy to insist that their children sit down and eat a proper family meal. As a result, convenience food becomes the line of least resistance, as you succumb to the tyranny of the take-away.

Even the kitchen itself – once considered to be the heart of the home – is changing radically. In the United States, new houses and yuppie apartments are being built today that don't even have a cooker in their mini-kitchens, just a microwave. Your kitchen can – and should – be a haven where you can regenerate your energy, use your creative talents, and produce wonderful food that looks good, tastes good, and does you and your family good – with a minimum of time and effort. At the end of a long, stressful day, half an hour spent in the kitchen preparing a meal can be the best of all therapies.

Fast food doesn't have to mean poor food. Fast food can be good food – Superfast Food. *Superfast Foods* will show you how. Discover the abundance of great convenience foods that are available. Learn how to make the most of the tinned, dried, and frozen foods that still supply the essential nutrients you and your family need. In *Superfast Foods* you'll find all you need to know about feeding your family quickly and well. You'll be able to take the relentless drudgery out of cooking, and learn how to get the best nutritional value for money. You'll even have the children eating healthier food without a murmur. Once you've found out for yourself how quick and easy cooking Superfast Foods can be, you'll also discover something that our grandmothers knew in more leisured times – that preparing, serving, and sitting down to good food with the ones you love can be the most deeply rewarding of pleasures.

FAST FOOD v. SUPERFAST FOOD

There is nothing wrong with enjoying a burger and fries, fish and chips, or a take-away from your local Indian, Chinese, or Mexican restaurant – as long as your staple diet is a healthy one, and the take-away is an occasional treat. Unfortunately, the number of fast-food outlets is rocketing, and so is the number of people who depend on take-away foods for most of their meals. A recent government survey in Great Britain found that an average of 27 per cent of food energy was consumed outside the home – more than a quarter of all the calories eaten by the average person, in other words. This trend is alarming, because, in the words of the survey's authors, "Food eaten out of the home contained a lower proportion of protein than the diet as a whole, and contained more sugars and less fibre, iron and vitamins per unit energy than all foods consumed by the sample."

In the United States, on any day of the week and in any month of the year, one person in five will eat at a fast-food restaurant. And every second of that day, an estimated 200 people in the United States will order one or more hamburgers. A three-day study of the eating habits of 3,500 people, carried out in 1987 by the United States Department of Agriculture, came to much the same conclusion as the authors of the British survey. Calorie for calorie, foods eaten away from home had more fat, and less protein, calcium, vitamin A, vitamins B1, B2, and B6, and vitamin C than food eaten in the home. If the customers of fast-food restaurants ate wisely and well when at home, these deficiencies would matter less. But in the British survey, the worst-off among those studied still got many of their calories from food eaten outside the home, and generally their diets were nutritionally borderline, if not deficient in vital nutrients. Therefore, those whose nutritional needs are the most pressing are those getting the worst food. A British supermarket survey of family eating habits found that the worst-off families were spending around 30 per cent a head less each week on food, than the better-off. The difference, however, in how they spent their money was most revealing. The better-off spent almost 150 per cent more than the worse-off on green vegetables, 112 per cent more on fruit, and 70 per cent more on fish. They spent, by contrast, 95 per cent less on potatoes, 32 per cent less on sugar and jams, and 22 per cent less on fats. With the exception of potatoes – one of the great Superfoods, when they're not swimming in fat – the better-off people in the survey got it right, and the worse-off got it wrong, spending most of their money on the least healthy foods.

In the table below, compare the two sets of menus for a whole day's eating. On the left is a typical day of convenience food, as shown in dozens of surveys. On the right is the Superfast Food menu.

A DAY OF FAST FOOD	A DAY OF SUPERFAST FOOD
Breakfast Sugar-coated cornflakes with milk. Toasted white bread with butter and jam. Cup of tea with two teaspoons of sugar.	**Breakfast** Porridge. Two slices wholewheat toast with butter. Cup of tea.
Midday lunch break Sausage roll. Bar of chocolate. Cola drink.	**Midday lunch break** Egg and salad sandwich on wholewheat bread. Banana.
Tea time Cup of tea with two teaspoons of sugar. Chocolate digestives.	**Tea time** Cup of tea. Two wholewheat digestive biscuits.
Evening meal Take-away burger and chips. Apple pie with a scoop of ice cream. Milkshake.	**Evening meal** Bowl of thick vegetable soup from a can or carton. Grilled steak with grilled tomatoes, mashed potatoes, and broccoli. Plain yogurt served with a tablespoonful each of sunflower seeds and honey.

We asked a leading nutritionist to analyse the two diets, and compare the results with the recommended intake for all nutrients, based on the daily requirements of a moderately active woman, aged 19–50. This is what she found. The fast-food diet was below the recommended intake levels for vitamin C, vitamin E, iron, selenium, zinc, folic acid, magnesium, and fibre – providing less than half the vital quantity for most, and only one third of the fibre. It was well above the recommended intake of calories and total fat. Fifty per cent of the calories came from carbohydrates, 40 per cent from fat, and 10 per cent from protein: too many from the fat and too few from the protein.

The Superfast Food diet met, or surpassed, the recommended levels of nutrient intake for all the vitamins, minerals, and micronutrients needed for healthy living, except for fibre, where it was 10 per cent short of the ideal amount, though still double that provided by the diet of fast food. The proportion of calories from carbohydrates is 50 per cent, from protein, 20 per cent, and from fat, 30 per cent – the ideal calorie distribution. It was below the recommended maximum intake for fats, salt, and sugar. It need take only minutes longer to prepare good fast food than bad. We compared the menus, meal by meal:

Breakfast

If you use instant porridge, you can make it in little more than the time it takes to boil a small panful of water – about two or three minutes.

Midday lunch break

You don't need to queue any longer for a wholewheat sandwich than for a sausage roll – a wholewheat sandwich doesn't have to be heated up, either.

Evening meal

It will take you under 30 minutes to prepare the Superfast Food evening meal main course. Put on the kettle. Heat the soup. Peel and dice the potatoes, and put them in a pan. Cover with the boiling water, and put them on to cook. Clean and halve the tomatoes. Brush the steak with a little olive oil, season, and put it under a hot grill with the tomatoes. Put the broccoli on to cook in a little boiling water. After five minutes, turn the steak, strain and mash the potatoes, strain the broccoli, and sit down to a delicious, fast meal. How long does it take to stir sunflower seeds and honey into some yogurt? Admittedly, you don't have to make the burger and chips yourself, but if you take into account the time spent getting to the take-away restaurant and standing in the queue, then you are not saving any time by eating badly.

DOESN'T HEALTHY EATING COST A FORTUNE?

Suppose you buy 500 g (1 lb) of fresh new potatoes at the greengrocer, and then buy the same weight of potato crisps. You will find that you pay around 19 times more for the crisps, and for your money you'll be getting an unhealthy dose of fat, salt, and maybe a bunch of chemicals, too. This is the first lesson in understanding food value for money – the less anybody has done to the food you buy, the cheaper it is. A potato is grown and harvested by the farmer, and transported to the wholesaler, who distributes it to the retailer where you buy it – all within as little as 24 hours. So four sets of people are making a living from your potato, and you're eating it soon after harvesting, when it is still richly nutritious. Turn the potato into crisps, and you not only have the farmer, and the transporter to get it to the factory, but you also have to add on to the price of the crisps the cost of manufacture, packaging, delivery to another wholesaler, and delivery to the retailer. What's more, somebody has to pay for all that prime-time television advertising. Guess who?

Eating healthily doesn't have to cost a fortune. In terms of nutrition, more expensive certainly doesn't mean more valuable. The cheapest shin of beef is no less nutritious than a Chateaubriand steak; and common, locally grown vegetables will actually be fresher and more vitamin-rich than expensive, much-travelled, out-of-season alternatives. Try to buy as many fresh, unpackaged, unprocessed foods as possible. Not only will they cost much less than pre-packed foods, but they will also be considerably fresher, and thus a better buy nutritionally. Befriend your local butcher, greengrocer, and fishmonger. They will be able to advise you on how to cook unfamiliar joints, vegetables, or fish, which may be the cheapest buy of the day. This is even more important if you're shopping just for one person, since many prepacked foods are designed for a minimum of two people.

Choose staple foods from the A–Z of Superfoods *(see pages 167–173)*. Get into the habit of planning meals two or three days ahead. Learn to be resourceful with leftovers. Resist the almost-irresistible impulse buys, as you push the supermarket trolley between shelves groaning with tempting delights. Most important of all, learn to be creative and experimental in your kitchen. If you do not have every single ingredient in a recipe, you can find a substitute – short of total incineration, you have to do something extremely awful to render food inedible. You will soon discover that you don't have to spend a great deal of money to eat healthily. We costed our two sets of menus for a whole day's eating *(see page 15)*, buying all of the items at the same snack bars, or supermarket. Eating the healthy Superfast Food menus actually cost 1½ per cent less than the junk food menus.

In the affluent Western World, those struggling to survive on the lowest incomes often spend their food budget in the worst way. Look into their shopping trolleys, and you'll find that they buy, for example, white bread because it's cheaper than wholemeal, margarine because it's cheaper than butter, and packets of instant desserts because they think they're cheaper than fresh fruit. People are convinced that they can't afford "real" food, still less healthy food, but the same people regularly spend money at the fish and chip shop, the pie shop, the hamburger restaurant, and the Indian or Chinese take-away. An enormous amount of money is spent on junk food. Among the top 20 best-selling foodstuffs in Britain in 1990, Coca-Cola came second, with a market worth £176 million; a brand of white sugar was third (£139 million); a brand of potato crisps ninth (£90 million); and a chocolate bar was fourteenth (£80 million). Shopping and eating in Sydney offers an almost unbelievable choice of the finest fish, fruit, and vegetables, and ethnic restaurants from every corner of the world. But travel to the Atherton Tablelands – the fruit basket of north Queensland – and most of the restaurants are greasy spoons serving pie and chips and fruit salads from syrup-laden tins.

Nutritionally, such foods contribute almost nothing but calories. It is the poorest sector of the community that not only eats worst in nutritional terms, but also fares worst in terms of illness and disease. While social deprivation and poor housing are major factors affecting public health, inadequate and unbalanced eating lies at the root of a huge proportion of illnesses affecting the poorest sector of Western societies. Before you say, "My diet is fine", or, "I wouldn't feed my family on that rubbish", keep a notebook for one week, and faithfully record every single item of food or drink that goes into your mouth, and get your family to do the same. At the end of the week, add up just how much high-fat, high-sugar, and low-nutrient foods and drinks have come your way. Count every biscuit, sweet, chocolate, sweet fizzy drink, greasy take-away, packet of crisps, ice-cream dessert, bag of chips, pork pie, and sausage roll that you have bought. Then work out how much they've cost you.

The more knowledgable you are about nutrition, the easier it is to make good choices of food for yourself and your family. A burger and French fries, or a helping of the best fish and chips in the neighbourhood, are fun food once in a while. Everybody likes a bar of chocolate now and then. In a heatwave, what can be more delicious than a good ice cream? It is when these foods become your staple diet, however, and when they crowd the good, health-building foods out of your budget, that your health will suffer. This is the price you're paying.

ALL YOU'LL EVER NEED TO KNOW ABOUT NUTRITION

Your great-grandmother may never have heard the word nutrition. She didn't know a carbohydrate from a protein, a good fat from a bad fat, or a vitamin from a mineral. In spite of this, she raised your grandmother, who raised your mother, who raised you. How on earth did she do it without the help of nutrition experts, with their lists and diagrams? Simple – common sense. She served foods that were fresh and in season, and she planned good, square meals with a wide range of ingredients, which the family sat down to, and enjoyed together. Nutritionists have been arguing about exactly what we should be eating ever since the first vitamin was discovered in the early years of this century. Today, however, there is nearly complete agreement throughout the world. The rules of sound nutrition can be summed up quite simply:

- **Eat plenty of fresh fruit and vegetables**

- **Eat a large variety of foods**

- **Eat more fibre**

- **Eat less fat**

- **Eat less sugar**

- **Eat less salt**

Twenty years ago, a handful of orthodox scientists raised the alarm about links between the diet of Western civilization and the diseases of affluence. They were branded scaremongers by the medical establishment and the food industry. Today, thanks to the weight of the World Health Organization, government bodies, and the avant-garde of the medical world, things are changing, if slowly. If you're worried about your lack of nutritional knowledge, you can relax – here is all you need to know.

WHAT'S WHAT IN FOOD

Carbohydrates

Carbohydrates occur in grains, such as wheat and rice, pulses, such as beans and lentils, and some root vegetables, such as potatoes, parsnips, and yams. These are often referred to as "complex carbohydrates". All you need to know is that foods like wholemeal bread, brown rice, certain breakfast cereals (porridge, shredded wheat, unsweetened muesli), pasta, beans, and potatoes, are all wholesome. They are good because they provide energy and a wide range of nutrients. They are generally inexpensive and bulky, and traditional, healthy diets all over the world are based largely on grains and pulses.

Confusingly, sugars are also carbohydrates, and these are not good for you, especially if they supply most of the energy in your diet. Refined sugars, like sucrose, glucose, dextrose, and maltose are used in massive quantities in processed foods, including savoury products, such as baked beans and tomato soup. You can often find three or four of them listed in the ingredients on food packets. These sugars do not need processing by the body, and are absorbed straight into the bloodstream, stimulating the pancreas to produce excess insulin. The sugars that your body produces from complex carbohydrates do not have this effect. Honey has been used as a sweetener since the first beehive was found, and, used in sensible amounts, it is far preferable as a sweetener than any form of sugar. Honey also contains traces of many nutrients.

Until the mid-19th century, white, refined wheat flour was unknown, and until early this century, most of the rice eaten around the world was unpolished, brown rice. What is "refined" out of wheat and rice is most of the goodness. Study the table overleaf, and you will see which nutrients you're missing when you eat bread made from white flour, instead of an honest wholemeal loaf. In many countries in the West, including Britain, the United States, Canada, Australia, and New Zealand, certain of these nutrients must by law be added back to the flour before it is baked into bread, but many vital nutrients are not.

NUTRITIONAL BREAKDOWN OF 100 g/3½ oz WHEAT FLOUR

	Wholemeal Flour	White Flour (self-raising)
Protein	12.7 g	9.4 g
Dietary fibre	8.6 g	3.6 g
Potassium	340 mg	150 mg
Magnesium	120 mg	20 mg
Iron	3.9 mg	2.0 mg
Calcium	38 mg	140 mg
Sodium	3.0 mg	3.0 mg
Zinc	2.9 mg	0.6 mg
Copper	0.45 mg	0.45 mg
Vitamin E	1.4 mg	0.3 mg
B vitamins:		
Folic acid	57 mg	22 mg
Biotin	7 mg	1 mg
Nicotinic acid	8.2 mg	3.6 mg
Pantothenic acid	0.8 mg	0.3 mg
Pyridoxine	0.50 mg	0.15 mg
Thiamin	0.47 mg	0.31 mg
Riboflavin	0.09 mg	0.03 mg
Niacin	5.7 mg	1.7 mg

1 g = 0.035 oz   1,000 mg = 1 g

Fat

Fat is a nutritional minefield, with bitter battles raging over it. You are probably hopelessly confused by the conflicting advice you see in the press, in full-page advertisements for certain brands of margarine, or in promotions paid for by the dairy industry. Owing to modern, intensive rearing methods, factory farming, and the vast meat-processing and fast-food industries, most people in the West today consume unacceptably high levels of animal fat. For much the same reasons, most people are not getting enough of the essential fatty acids found in seeds, nuts, whole grains, some vegetables, and oily fish.

Many people – especially women – believe that a low-fat diet means a no-fat diet. Consequently, they are missing out on almost all of the vital fats. Two fat-facts to note: firstly, all fats and oils contain the same number of calories by weight, unless they are fat-reduced factory products. Secondly, the simple division into the "good" polyunsaturated fats and the "bad" saturated fats is highly misleading. Foods that are as simple as nature intended them to be should be the rule rather than the exception. Most polyunsaturated margarine is a highly processed, unnatural foodstuff that contains trans fatty acids, which appear to be decidedly unhealthy. Natural butter, on the other hand, if used in moderation, is a useful source of vitamins A, D, and E.

We now know what every Mediterranean peasant has always known: that extra-virgin olive oil is a wonderful foundation on which to build your daily diet, and the best oil for your health – especially if it is combined with plenty of garlic and a glass of red wine a day. This is hardly surprising. Extra-virgin olive oil is obtained by a simple pressure process, and contains the natural goodness to be found in the olive. The consumption of vegetable oils (such as sunflower, safflower, and corn oil) for cooking has rocketed this century. Many of them, however, are heavily processed – bleached, deodorized, and refined – to turn them into the near-tasteless products you buy. Consequently, there is little of the natural goodness of the sunflower, the safflower, or the corn left in them.

REDUCE YOUR FAT INTAKE

1. Remove all visible fat from meat and poultry before cooking.

2. Save meat products, such as sausages, paté, meat pies, pasties, salami, and bacon for occasional treats – they provide up to 85 per cent of their calories from fat.

3. Watch out for the hidden fats. When you eat a small packet of potato crisps, up to two-thirds of its weight may be potato – the other third is fat. French fries are approximately 50 per cent fat. Most cakes, pastries, and biscuits are very high in fats. A 250 g (8 oz) burger can contain more than 50 g (2 oz) of fat, and a cheeseburger even more.

With Superfast Foods, your diet will be low in fat. Consequently, you can enjoy the pleasures of real butter, the occasional dollop of cream, and proper whole milk, instead of skimmed milk, which is nutritionally a very poor second cousin to the real thing.

Protein
Estimates of how much protein – body-building components – we need to keep us going have varied wildly, from the hefty 150 g (5 oz) a day proposed by 19th-century nutritionists – equivalent to the protein content of approximately 600 g (1¼ lb) of lean beef – to the more modest 55–90 g (2–3½ oz) for adults, recommended today.

24

How do you know whether you're getting enough protein? Simple. Unless you are following an extreme form of diet, such as a food-exclusion diet, or you are an exceptionally faddy eater, or an anorexic, it is almost impossible to be protein-deficient on an average, mixed diet. Quite the reverse: if you are eating eggs and bacon for breakfast, a pork pie at lunchtime, and meat and two vegetables in the evening, you may well be consuming far more protein than your body needs, and your kidneys will feel the strain. Furthermore, meat isn't the only good source of protein, as is obvious when you consider the world's millions of healthy vegetarians. For those with high blood pressure, it is useful to know that reducing your animal protein intake helps to bring it down. Fish, chicken, eggs, cheese, milk, beans, peas, nuts, grains, vegetables, and even some fruits all supply varying quantities of protein. The average Western adult gets around 66 per cent of his or her protein from meat, fish, eggs, cheese, and milk; 25 per cent from bread and other cereals; and 10 per cent from vegetables.

In spite of many doctors' opposition to vegetarianism, some of the healthiest races in the world never eat meat or animal products. The wisdom of centuries-old eating traditions helps these peoples balance their diets without even thinking about it. The old idea of first-class and second-class proteins, with meat belonging in the executive class, is now, thankfully, dying out. The only imperative for vegetarians is that they should get their protein from mixed sources, as in the traditional rice and peas of the West Indies, for example, the rice and lentils of the Middle East, the pasta and beans of Italy, and the rice and dal of India. It is virtually impossible, however, to be an adult vegan – avoiding eggs and all milk products – without supplementing the diet with B vitamins, and it is irresponsibly risky to bring up a child as a vegan unless you are extremely well-informed, and give the child dietary supplements.

Fibre

Fibre occurs in whole grains, pulses, vegetables, fruits, and seeds. A hundred years ago nobody needed to worry about fibre – it was naturally present in their daily bread, cereals, and vegetables. There is now a huge body of evidence to suggest that when your diet is deficient in fibre, you are likely to suffer from a whole range of digestive nasties – from constipation to cancer of the bowel. As well as benefiting the digestive system, certain forms of fibre – especially the type in oats, barley, and beans – help the body eliminate excess cholesterol, and consequently protect the heart and circulatory system.

Vitamins and Minerals

Even a qualified nutritionist would need a computer to work out how many of your daily vitamin and mineral needs will be met by a particular diet or foodstuff. Without burdening you with an incomprehensible array of numbers, here are some simple guidelines to ensure that you obtain all of your vitamin and mineral requirements.

1. The fresher the fruit and vegetables you eat, the better they are for you. Much of their goodness starts to disappear the moment they are picked. The loss of vitamin C is increased by storage, handling, bruising, and preparation. Heat is the final enemy of vitamin C. The most nutritious way of eating many vegetables and most fruit is raw. Try one meal a day of nothing but raw foods – wonderful fruit, delicious salads, a crunchy carrot or cauliflower, peppers, fennel, celery, and unroasted nuts. Keeping cooked vegetables warm will destroy what little vitamin C may be left. B vitamins and many minerals leach out into the cooking water, so cook vegetables in a minimum of water, for the shortest possible time.

2. Good, fresh produce is always the first choice when it comes to buying vegetables. Commercially frozen vegetables are also a good option, since they are harvested and frozen at their best, when their vitamin content is at its highest. They may lose some vitamin C, but they will contain more than vegetables that have spent a long time in transit, in the shop, or in your vegetable rack. Frozen vegetables are handy for the Superfast Foods cook, since they can turn a snack into a nutritious meal.

3. Discover nuts and seeds: they're not just for the budgie. Almonds, hazelnuts, walnuts, cashews, chestnuts, and sunflower, sesame, and pumpkin seeds are all available in supermarkets, and they're delicious. They also happen to be bursting with B vitamins, vitamin E, zinc, iron, protein, and fibre – the nutrients for their future growth into trees, shrubs and flowers. For suggestions on how to use them, refer to the A–Z of Superfoods *(see pages 167–173)*.

4. There are supernutrients and antinutrients. All the vitamins are essential for life, but some are supernutrients, such as beta-carotene, which is found in brightly coloured fruit and vegetables, and converted by the body into vitamins A, C, and E. The supernutrients are also known as antioxidants, the function of which is to mop up excess free radicals, which are the by-products of body chemistry. These are now known to be highly destructive to individual cells, and they can trigger cancer, heart disease, as well as many other serious disorders. Free radicals are also responsible for signs of the body's ageing process, such as wrinkles.

An ever-growing body of research has now established beyond doubt the key role of the antioxidants in keeping us healthy. Indeed, conventional nutritionists who as little as a decade ago were confidently asserting that the "average" diet supplied all our nutritional needs, are now urging us to increase our intake of fresh fruit and vegetables. The 1990 recommendation of the World Health Organization is that everyone should eat at least 400 g (14 oz) of a wide variety of fruit and vegetables – not including potatoes – daily. This confirms the wisdom of the health "cranks" who, a century ago, were saying just that. Eat a freshly made salad containing green leaves, red peppers, grated carrot, radishes, fennel, chopped parsley, and tomatoes, dressed with extra-virgin olive oil, and you're enjoying a mega-helping of the antioxidants.

Antinutrients are substances that either interfere with the body's absorption of nutrients, or destroy them. The much-touted bran, lavishly packed into cereals, or sprinkled into soup, can have a disastrous effect on the absorption of calcium, iron, and other minerals. Coffee, tea, and other caffeine carriers, such as cola and chocolate drinks can also lower the amount of iron that the body will absorb from food. Vitamin C, on the other hand, will maximize it, so if you must have coffee with your boiled egg (a good source of iron), have some orange juice as well. Refined sugars and alcohol drain the body's vitamin B reserves. Certain drugs also lower nutrient uptake or bodily stores of nutrients, among them antibiotics, the Pill, antidepressants, antacids, and laxatives. If you are taking any of these regularly, your diet should be especially good, and you should consider taking a simple vitamin supplement.

5. At least once a day, eat a home-cooked meal, at the table, not in front of the television, and not in a rush. This way of eating is good for your digestion, and results in your body getting more nutrients from the food. Not to mention the fact that you and your partner, your family, or your friends will gather around the table, and talk to each other – something which few people make time to do these days. If you can't manage a daily gathering around the dining table, resurrect the traditional Sunday lunch, or the Friday evening family feast. Such gatherings are often among our richest childhood memories, but how many of today's children will be able to look back on them?

THE SUPERFAST FOOD KITCHEN

Superfast Foods are only fast when you're organized. This is where a well-stocked, well-equipped kitchen is important. Even a tin of beans can take half an hour to prepare for eating if you can't find the tin-opener. Many of the Superfoods come in cans or packets, and if they're to hand, you can rustle up a dozen delicious, well-balanced meals in minutes, without ever stirring from your kitchen. Of course, when it comes to fruit, vegetables, and salads, fresh is best, but if you're at work until after closing time, or in too much of a hurry, or if you need to do the shopping in one weekly trip to the supermarket, then stock up with cans and freezer packs. Choose storable foods that still supply plenty of vitamins and beta-carotene, such as frozen vegetables. If the alternative is to eat old, wilting vegetables from the corner shop, then frozen ones will be a better nutritional option. The following are lists of essential Superfast Foods.

THE STORE CUPBOARD

Tinned Foods
Italian plum tomatoes – whole tomatoes are best, as the chopped or sieved ones often have other ingredients added.
Chickpeas.
Sugar-free baked beans.
Tuna.
Sardines.
Anchovies.
Salmon.
Pilchards.

Oils
Extra-virgin olive oil and plain olive oil.
Lighter oils, such as groundnut oil or sunflower oil.
Sesame oil for wok cooking.

Sauces and Condiments

Shoyu, or a naturally fermented soy sauce.

Worcestershire sauce.

White wine vinegar or cider vinegar.

Good mayonnaise.

Dijon and grainy mustards.

Salt – sea salt is incomparably superior in flavour to ordinary table salt.

Stock cubes or vegetable *bouillon* powder.

Condensed tomato purée in a tube.

Condensed anchovy essence.

Grains and Pasta

Wholewheat flour.

Brown rice – use the quick-cook kind if you're pushed for time.

Bulgur wheat, or burghul, can be eaten uncooked, so it's a perfect fast food.

Pasta – make sure it's made from 100 per cent durum wheat, since other varieties can become flabby while cooking.

Herbs

Fresh herbs can give a terrific boost to your cooking. More and more supermarkets sell pots of fresh herbs to grow on the kitchen windowsill. Parsley, mint, chives, and basil should always be used fresh, while rosemary, sage, oregano, thyme, and bay leaves are also good dried.

Dried herbs and spices can deteriorate fast in storage. They are best kept in the dark, and replaced regularly. Stale herbs and spices do nothing for your cooking.

Miscellaneous

Black olives – you can buy them loose, transfer them to a small jar, and cover them with extra-virgin olive oil and a sprinkling of herbs.

Artichoke hearts in olive oil – a useful stand-by for pasta sauces.

Dried fruit – apricots, prunes, raisins, and sultanas. Almost all prunes and apricots are preserved with sulphur dioxide, and need to be carefully washed before use.

Spices

Cayenne pepper or crushed, dried whole chillies.

Paprika.

Whole nutmeg.

Black peppercorns – ready-ground pepper is a useful stand-by, but the flavour is not as good.

Cinnamon sticks and ground cinnamon.

Coriander and cumin, both ground – renew them when they lose their aroma.

Whole cloves.

Ground ginger, and preserved ginger pieces in syrup – a teaspoonful or so of the syrup can spice up sauces and puddings.

Turmeric.

A good ready-made curry powder, mild or hot, according to your preference. Don't keep it for too long, however, since it loses its flavour rapidly.

THE REFRIGERATOR

Cheese

Piece of good-quality Cheddar cheese.

Piece of fresh Parmesan cheese – ready-grated Parmesan is tastless.

Fromage frais.

Salads and Vegetables

Iceberg lettuce keeps well, so it is a good salad stand-by.

Carrots.

Sun-dried tomatoes in olive oil, once a luxury, can now be bought quite inexpensively in many supermarkets. Use them up quickly.

Nuts

Have a selection of almonds, walnuts, cashews, and brazils. Since nuts can turn rancid on exposure to air, owing to their high fat content, buy small packets of whole nuts, and use them up quickly.

Seeds

Once opened, seeds should always be stored in jars in the fridge. They can turn rancid if left for too long.

Sunflower seeds – buy small packets, and use them up quickly.

Sesame seeds.

Miscellaneous

Milk.

Small carton of single cream.

Butter.

Plain yogurt.

Greek yogurt.

Eggs.

Smoked streaky bacon – buy small amounts at a time, and pay attention to the use-by dates.

Whole lemon.

Fresh parsley.

THE FREEZER

Bread

Wholewheat sliced loaf for toasting.

Wholewheat or granary rolls.

Wholewheat pitas.

Vegetables

Spinach – puréed or in leaf form. Some brands come in useful packets with individual portions.

Sweetcorn.

French beans.

Petits pois.

Broccoli.

Stew packets of mixed vegetables. These can form the basis of a quick, nourishing soup.

Stir-fry vegetables – various combinations are available.

Fish

Fillets – or other cuts of firm white fish – can be cooked from frozen.

Packets of shrimps or prawns.

Fish stock – this can make all the difference to a quick fish soup.

Fruit

Summer fruits – keep a mixture of blackcurrants, redcurrants, raspberries, and bilberries. A spoonful of these fruits transforms a helping of Greek yogurt into a luxury dessert.

Frozen concentrated orange juice is useful as a base for fruit salads, or for adding to plain yogurt.

THE VEGETABLE RACK AND FRUIT BOWL

Vegetables

Potatoes and onions – store them in brown paper bags, away from light, and use them before they start to sprout.

Garlic – storing garlic in a porous earthenware container with ventilation holes will keep it in good condition.

Fruit

Apples.

Oranges.

Grapefruit – the pink-fleshed variety, extra-rich in beta-carotene, makes a delicious breakfast.

EQUIPPING THE SUPERFAST FOOD KITCHEN

If you're always pushed for time, money spent on equipping your kitchen for the preparation of super-quick meals is money very well spent. If your time is money, you can't afford not to have the essential equipment listed here.

Stainless steel saucepans
Buy the best set you can afford – they'll last you a lifetime. You can fry onions and other vegetables for starting off soups and stews in the same pan you use to cook the dish, instead of having to use a separate pan – an important time saver. Avoid aluminium pans, as these can be a health hazard – excess aluminium intake has been linked with Alzheimer's Disease. If you can't replace yours immediately, then avoid cooking acidic foods, such as fruit in them.

Non-stick saucepan You will need this for making sauces, scrambling eggs, and heating milk.

Non-stick frying pans If possible, have two: a smaller one is good for making omelettes. Make sure you use a non-stick slice with them.

Wok This is indispensable for stir-fry dishes, which are quick, tasty, and very healthy. See the recipes on pages 90, 101, and 108.

Hob-to-oven casseroles are useful for dishes that have to be started off on the hob, but can then be transferred to the oven.

Set of ovenproof dishes in ovenproof china or earthenware – these are useful for preparing gratin dishes, vegetables, and bakes.

Colanders One of your colanders should be heat-proof (steel or enamel), then it can double as a steamer, with a saucepan lid on top.

Salad spinner This makes it possible for even the busiest cook to have a perfectly dry, fresh, green salad every day.

Sharp kitchen knives It is useful to have three or four, including at least one with a serrated blade, for slicing soft foods, such as tomatoes.

Wooden chopping boards – in various sizes. Once a week, pour boiling water over them, and give them a good scrub.

Wooden spoons Be sure to have plenty of these, in different sizes. Many cooks have one or two cherished wooden spoons, which they couldn't do without, for making a sauce or a mayonnaise.

Spatula, slotted spoon, and fish-slice that you can use with non-stick pans.

Bowls – in china or pyrex, for mixing and storage.

Handled sieves

Lidded glass or perspex containers – for storing fresh herbs and leftovers in the fridge.

Measuring jugs You will find it helpful to have a small pyrex jug for making sauces, as well as a bigger plastic one.

Set of kitchen scales

Pepper mill – one of those items that it is worth spending a little more on. Test them, and choose one that does a good grinding job.

Grater The square kind with different-sized graters on each side is the most useful. Italian cylindrical cheese graters are very quick to use.

INDISPENSABLES FOR THE KITCHEN DRAWER

Potato peeler

Potato masher

Kitchen scissors – tough enough to cope with bacon rind, and to cut up pieces of chicken.

Small whisk

Garlic crusher

Knife sharpener

Good tin-opener

Italian pasta-server This is an ingenious scoop with toothed sides for dishing out pasta. It also conveys boiled eggs from pan to egg cup without a spill.

Mini-stapler – handy for resealing freezer packets.

GOOD GADGETS

Some gadgets are worth their weight in caviar to the harassed cook, and one such piece of equipment is a food processor. In the Superfast Food kitchen, a food processor is indispensable for mincing meat, making breadcrumbs, grating vegetables, puréeing soups, and mixing batters, to mention just a few of its myriad uses. You will also find the following very useful:

Electric kettle Make sure it has a switch-off mechanism.

Electric toaster

Mandoline If you don't have a food processor, this French device makes fast work of slicing vegetables into different thicknesses.

Juice extractor With a good juicer you can prepare in minutes a delicious mega-dose of fresh, natural goodness – especially of the vital antioxidant vitamins. See pages 162–163 for ideas for drinks.

Mouli-légumes This non-electrical French gadget allows you to blend and sieve at the same time, and produces soups with a much more interesting texture than either a blender or a food processor.

Herb cutter This comprises a shallow, wooden bowl, with a handled, half-moon blade – an excellent device for chopping herbs swiftly and thoroughly, without crushing them to a purée.

TIMESAVING TIPS IN THE KITCHEN

• Before you start on any of the recipes in this book, read the recipe through, and make sure that you have all of the ingredients to hand, and every bit of equipment.

• Preheat the oven or grill, and put the kettle on, or boil up a panful of water in advance, if you are going to need them.

• Have plenty of kitchen paper handy to blot dry meat, fish, and vegetables after cleaning them, to drain excess fat from fried foods, to wipe out frying pans, and to mop up spills.

• Clutter slows down cooking: tidy waste into the bin as you work.

• Make a supply of salad dressing *(see page 143)*, and store it in a tightly sealed bottle – porcelain-capped bottles are ideal – in a cool, dark place. It will double as a ready-made marinade for chicken and fish.

• Finely chop a quantity of parsley – you can do this in a food processor – and freeze it. You can then use it a little at a time.

• When you are making pasta, here is how to have the dish to serve it in piping-hot, without having to use the oven. Stand a colander in the serving dish in the sink, and have a tea-towel to hand. When the pasta is cooked, drain it into the colander, pick up the colander and deposit it on the sauce-pan to allow it to finish draining. Tip the hot pasta water out of the serving dish, and wipe the dish dry.

• To skin tomatoes and peaches, put them in a bowl, and cover them with boiling water. Test the skin of one with the tip of a knife, and when it is ready to slide off, empty the bowl.

• To remove the bitter juices from sliced aubergines, pour boiling water over them. This saves time otherwise spent salting and draining them.

• To skin a clove of garlic quickly, crush it under the blade of a knife.

• Remove the crusts from whole-wheat bread that is beginning to go stale, and turn it into crumbs in the food processor. You can store the crumbs in the freezer in a carton with a lid, and use them for rissoles and burgers, or for coating fish. Breadcrumbs defrost in minutes.

• Keep three or four medicine-sized bottles containing olive oil, to which you can add a variety of surplus herbs and spices. This way you have ready-made flavoured oils to hand – use garlic and chillies for a Mexican marinade, rosemary and tarragon for chicken dishes, dill for fish, and oregano for a Mediterranean flavour.

• Keep a list in a prominent place of essential store cupboard items – peppercorns, tomato purée, canned tomatoes, stock cubes – that are running low, so that you can replace them before they run out.

SUPERFAST FOODS FOR ALL – NINE CASE STUDIES

Even if you are following the nutritional guidelines, as explained in
All You'll Ever Need to Know about Nutrition *(see pages 19–26)*, there
are times in all our lives that make extra nutritional demands on us.
These include periods of growth, the turbulent teens, the unpredictable
student years, and times when you have to cope with situations, such
as pregnancy and motherhood, bringing up a family, the demands of a
stressful job, the menopause, and retirement. In any of these situations,
you'll be healthier, your spirits will be more buoyant, and you'll
weather the tough times better if you eat Superfoods, rich in all the
nutrients you need to deal with them. It is absolutely certain that unless
you are eating well at these times, you will lack the vitality and
resilience to cope.

Here are nine case studies of people at different periods of life – at
least one should be familiar to you. Each incudes a list of the
Superfoods that possess the nutrients most needed, and some simple
menus for Superfast Food main meals that supply them.

CHILDREN

"I'm late home from work, the seven-year-old has to be at the gym, the nine-year-old has a rehearsal for the school play, and the baby's screaming. As usual, I'm cook, bottle washer, and chauffeur. Mum can't stay and help, and I haven't had time to stop off at the supermarket."

What active children need is lots of energy from complex carbohydrates, such as potatoes and brown rice, modest amounts of protein for growth, preferably from chicken, fish, and wholegrain cereals, and plenty of vitamins and minerals from fresh fruit, vegetables, and salads. They also need calcium from milk – full-fat milk, not skimmed – yogurt, mild cheese, such as cottage cheese, green vegetables, and oily fish, like sardines, tuna, and salmon. Children need plenty of magnesium – a mineral we hear little about – which is supplied by whole grains, nuts, and dark green, leafy vegetables.

Contrary to what they would have you believe, babyfood manufacturers do not know more about feeding children than you do. Nor is their food any more hygienic or better than the products of your own kitchen. Too often, babyfood is little more than bland mush, while many of the puddings and drinks aimed at toddlers contain appallingly high levels of sugar. If small children get used to these bland, sweet tastes as a daily experience, you'll have an uphill struggle getting them to enjoy anything you prepare yourself. So the sooner you start dishing up real food to your children, the sooner they'll begin to appreciate it. As often as possible, let them join the adults around the dinner table so that they learn to enjoy good food. Italian parents introduce even their smallest children to the wonderful flavours of the Mediterranean kitchen. Why not follow suit?

FEED YOUR CHILDREN SIMPLE FOOD

Children don't need fancy food. What's more, since they are deeply conservative by nature, and suspicious of all change, they'll happily eat the same foods over and over again, once they decide they like them.

Most children love roast chicken, hot or cold. Try pieces of cold roast chicken in a salad. Iceberg lettuce is ideal, and a wonderful way to introduce children to salads: break it into small pieces, add chunks of tomatoes, some cress, and dress it with a spoonful of creamy mayonnaise. Alternatively, make fingers of chicken breast dipped in egg and breadcrumbs, and fried or grilled with tomatoes and onion.

Two fishy meals for the children that can be quickly prepared from cans in the store cupboard are fishcakes made with canned salmon or tuna, mixed with some cooked potatoes (this is a good way of using up leftover potatoes), and tuna and bean salad. Try giving them sardines on toast, finished under a hot grill for a minute or two, or some white fish, cooked in milk with potatoes, and gratinéed.

What child can resist a boiled egg with soldiers? The soldiers should be made from wholewheat toast, which supplies more all-round goodness in the form of iron, potassium, fibre, and vitamin E, than white bread – see the table on page 22.

Getting young children to eat their greens or salads may be difficult, and the task is not helped by insecurity or diffidence on your part, which they easily pick up on. Don't be apologetic or anxious – put the food in front of them, and let them get on with it. Popeye is still encouraging thousands of children to eat up their spinach. They'll find it delicious, puréed with a little butter and nutmeg, and served with triangles of fried wholewheat bread. Broccoli and cauliflower can be lightly steamed, mashed up with a beaten egg, sprinkled with cheese, and grilled for a couple of minutes.

Be sure to give them plenty of raw fruit in season. Most children love little fruit salads, made from apples, bananas, sweet, ripe pears, oranges and tangerines, grapes, sweet fresh pineapple, strawberries, raspberries, or cherries. Bananas can be mashed up with yogurt, or made into nourishing drinks with a blender *(see page 161)*. A baked apple, stuffed with raisins and a little honey, and eaten with creamy Greek yogurt, is a wonderful winter pudding. For a deliciously different breakfast, dried apricots, apples, and prunes can be soaked overnight – just wash them and pour boiling water over them – and eaten with plain yogurt. Keep a supply of frozen summer fruits, such as redcurrants, blackcurrants, raspberries, and bilberries. Heat a tablespoonful of them in a saucepan until the juice begins to run, and stir them into some plain or Greek yogurt. The result is much tastier than artificially flavoured yogurts.

Soft drinks are a major source of excess sugar in children's diets. The average can of fizzy drink contains anything from eight to twelve teaspoonfuls of sugar. Soft drinks and other high-sugar foods are advertised heavily during children's television with the result that the invisible sugar consumed in processed foods has risen steadily over the last decade. Your children never need sugar added to food: all it supplies are empty calories. By the tender age of two or three, however, many children are already little sugar junkies, hooked for life on the stuff that is plugged constantly on the television they watch. When your children are thirsty, offer them water, a glass of milk, or – as a treat – pure fruit juice diluted with water.

Sooner or later, you'll have a sick child on your hands. Whether they catch a streaming cold, an odd bug, or a more serious childhood illness, such as chickenpox or mumps, your children will not be very hungry at these times. What is important, though, is that they have plenty of fluids and easy-to-digest, simple, nutritious foods. Give them liquidized soups, and high-energy drinks, made in the blender. Choose from the traditional sick-room foods – scrambled eggs, junket, real custard, porridge, yeast- or meat-extract drinks, milky drinks, and fruits, like grapes and apples, peeled and cut into segments, and bananas, mashed with a little cream and honey. Stomach upsets need the BRAT diet – bananas, rice, apples, and toast, and plenty of water to drink. The toast should be wholewheat and plain; the rice just plainly boiled.

SUPERFOODS
FOR CHILDREN

Bananas are a highly nutritious convenience food, packed with goodness. They have lots of potassium and a good helping of fibre.

Blackcurrants contain plenty of vitamin C and beta-carotene. Serve them fresh when possible, and keep reserves in the freezer for treats.

Broccoli and other dark green vegetables are rich in nutrients, including magnesium, which helps build healthy bone and muscle.

Chicken One of the most versatile foods, and a good source of protein, chicken is popular with children because of its bland flavour.

Eggs One of nature's most popular convenience foods, eggs are an excellent source of iron, in which many children's diets are deficient.

Milk Whole milk is an excellent source of nutrients in a child's diet, since it contains protein, calcium, and vitamins A, D, and E.

Oats pack a terrific nutritional punch. They contain plenty of protein, B vitamins, and the minerals needed to build strong bones and teeth.

Sunflower seeds Another great nutritional package, these are rich in minerals and good polyunsaturated fats.

Yogurt Like milk, yogurt supplies calcium, and it can help combat children's digestive infections.

MENUS
FOR CHILDREN

MONDAY
Tomato Risotto (p.118) with iceberg lettuce salad.
Fingers of carrot and celery.
Apple.

TUESDAY
Fishcakes (p.97) with Quick Tomato and Olive Sauce (p.144).
Steamed courgettes with butter and plenty of chopped parsley.

WEDNESDAY
Marlene's Tuna Pasta (p.121).
Mixed green salad with toasted sunflower seeds and
mayonnaise dressing.
Wholewheat roll.
Yogurt with honey and mixed nuts.

THURSDAY
Bread and Cheese Bake (p.86).
Puréed spinach.
Peach or pear.

FRIDAY
Grilled Fish with Cheese (p.93).
Broccoli steamed and tossed in a little olive oil and lemon.
Fingers of carrot and cucumber.
Ripe pear.

SATURDAY
Lamb Burgers (p.102) with Cauliflower Gratin I (p.131).
Summer fruits with plain yogurt.

SUNDAY
Roast chicken with baked potatoes and braised cabbage.
Toffee Bananas (p.157) with Greek yogurt.

TEENAGERS

"They've changed their minds again about this evening – now four of their friends are coming over for something to eat before they all go out dancing."

The teenage years are years of growth, development, and hormonal change, demanding the best possible nutrition. Years, too, when they'll need all the energy they can get, to help them enjoy the fun – and cope with the stresses – of their exciting, active lives.

It is especially important for teenagers to eat a proper breakfast. If they race to school every morning after no more than a cup of tea, the temptation to boost nose-diving blood sugar levels with mid-morning coffee or chocolate will be irresistible. Porridge is a great breakfast, and you can make it in two or three minutes. It will provide vital minerals, like iron, zinc, and calcium, and the nerve-fortifying B vitamins. Eat it with milk and a little honey.

If your teenagers' packed lunches consist of sandwiches, make these with wholewheat bread. For the filling, use hard-boiled egg, cheese, tuna, tinned sardines, or chicken for protein. Add lettuce leaves, cress, or watercress for greenery, plenty of chopped parsley – good for an unblemished skin – and a dollop of mayonnaise for the tastiest sandwiches ever. Include with the packed lunch a carton of plain yogurt or plain cottage cheese, a piece of fruit, such as a banana, an apple, or a pear, and mineral water to drink.

Make sure the evening meal includes a green vegetable, such as spinach, broccoli, kale, cabbage, or cauliflower. For interesting variations on the greens theme, see the recipes on pages 125–135. A salad, or at least one raw vegetable, is a must on the menu – a couple of carrots, scraped clean and cut into chunks, a crisp stick of celery, or slivers of red or yellow peppers. Or try that American favourite – spinach salad with mushrooms thinly sliced into it, and a creamy, garlicky, mayonnaise dressing.

If you want your children to eat well, rather than go to take-aways, you'll have to be ready to feed their friends, too, at short notice. This is when a well-stocked store cupboard, refrigerator, and freezer really come to the rescue. When your children do head for the hamburgers, cokes, and chips with the rest of the gang, remind them to sample the salad bar, and point out to them that one large milkshake contains eight teaspoons of sugar, and a king-sized cola drink has fourteen.

TEENAGE STRESS

To cope with the stresses of adolescence, teenagers need foods that are rich in B vitamins. These include wholegrain cereals, such as porridge oats, liver, meat, chicken, fish, and leafy green vegetables. Certain wholegrain foods, like brown rice and wholewheat bread also supply zinc, needed for growth and clear skin, iron for energy and mental staying power, and calcium and magnesium for strong bones.

Dietary surveys worldwide have shown up deficiencies of iron in the diet of children and teenagers, and females are especially at risk, because of menstruation. The chronic lack of energy that is one consequence of iron deficiency is widespread among teenagers today. Make sure that they get plenty of iron in their diet, not just from meat, but also from egg yolks, spinach, pulses, nuts, and seeds. Remember that drinking tea or coffee with a meal will lower the body's ability to absorb iron, while vitamin C, present in fruit juices, will boost it.

Excess weight can create appalling problems of insecurity and loss of confidence for teenagers. In despair, many of them will resort to drastic diets featuring little more than lettuce leaves and black coffee, which can be a serious danger to health. Whatever you do, don't let them cut down on the sensible foods they need for growth and energy. Instead, remind them that the key factors to weight gain are excess fat and sugar, and lots of both are found in their favourite snacks, such as burgers, sausages, salami, chips, crisps, and ice cream. Anorexia can sneak up on youngsters who become too obsessive about weight, and who start cutting out mineral-rich foods. The vital mineral here is zinc, a lack of which can destroy the appetite. Good sources are shrimps, crab meat, sardines, mackerel, liver, meat, wheatgerm from wholewheat bread, sesame and pumpkin seeds, cheese, and green vegetables.

Like excess weight, acne and other skin problems can cause agony to teenagers. Victims need to watch fat and sugar intake. Their best friend, though, is the colour green, which should always be on the menu, even if it's only a sprig of parsley. Green vegetables and herbs contain lots of beta-carotene, which our bodies process into vitamin A, vital for healthy skin. Green also indicates a high level of chlorophyll, which has a cleansing and nourishing effect on the skin, and protects it from infection.

SUPERFOODS
FOR TEENAGERS

Dates are nourishing and conveniently portable. Eat them for energy, the much-needed iron they supply, and their high potassium content.

Mackerel, fresh, smoked, or tinned, is a good source of healthy fats, protein, and vital minerals.

Oranges are high in vitamin C and beta-carotene, which help teenagers stand up to infection, and help keep the skin clear.

Parsley Rich in vitamins A and C, and iron, parsley is useful for all those with skin problems.

Porridge made from oatmeal is nutritious and easily digested. Oats are calming and restorative to the nervous system, partly on account of their calcium and magnesium content.

Pumpkin seeds are rich in B vitamins, iron, zinc, unsaturated fatty acids, and protein. Serve them toasted, or tossed in sesame seed oil.

Spinach is a Superfood for those with skin problems, owing to its high beta-carotene content. Its chlorophyll – the lifeblood of plants – helps counter anaemia, fatigue, and infection.

Turkey is high in protein, very low in saturated fat, and rich in zinc, a mineral vital for good health.

MENUS
FOR TEENAGERS

MONDAY

Presia's Eggs Bolognese (p.84) with steamed cauliflower tossed in
butter and plenty of chopped parsley.
Apple.

TUESDAY

Beef Stir-Fry (p.101) with French beans and a wholewheat roll.
Apple.

WEDNESDAY

Bean Casserole (p.116).
Salad of iceberg lettuce, radishes, spring onions, and parsley.
Baked Apples (p.159) with Greek yogurt.

THURSDAY

Pasta with Meatball and Tomato Sauce (p.122).
Tossed green salad with watercress and a mayonnaise dressing.
Peach or nectarine.

FRIDAY

Fish with Mushrooms (p.96).
Spinach purée.
Grated carrot salad with parsley and toasted sunflower seeds.
Orange or tangerine.

SATURDAY

Henri's Pita Pizza (p.150).
Crudités – carrots, cucumbers, and cauliflower florets –
with Quick Garlic Mayonnaise (p.144).
Summer fruits with yogurt.

SUNDAY

Mediterranean Chicken (p.111).
Baked potatoes.
Cabbage tossed in olive oil and lemon juice.
Red Plum Pudding (p.158) with Greek yogurt.

STUDENTS

"There are three lectures and a practical today. By the time I've finished studying in the library, the college canteen will be shut, and my grant has nearly run out."

You made it to college, you've got masses of new friends, you're enjoying your new-found independence, and you can enjoy talking into the small hours with nobody telling you to go to bed. It's probably the first time you've lived away from home, and, as well as the course work, you'll have to cope with the washing, the ironing, the shopping, and the cooking. How well prepared are you? To make the most of these exciting years, you'll need to be fit and full of energy, and your brain should be running on all cylinders.

Sadly, this is seldom the case. Few students have even the most rudimentary knowledge of how to eat well, let alone how to cook. Too often students end up snacking endlessly on bread and cheese, or high-sugar foods, and fill the gaps with take-aways and chips with little nutritional value. If this is you, you shouldn't be surprised if you are constantly lethargic, struggling to concentrate on your work, and liable to go down with every cold or bout of flu that's doing the rounds.

You do not have to be Anton Mosimann to master the art of healthy eating. Nor do you need a vast array of pots and pans, and other equipment. Even with a single burner, a couple of saucepans, a wok, and a slow-cooker – if you can persuade your parents to donate it – you can live like a prince on very little money. What you must eat are foods that supply masses of energy, enough protein for growth and repair, the essential fatty acids for your brain, and vitamins and minerals to boost your resistance, and prevent disease.

This book won't change overnight the lifestyle of a generation of students, but if it persuades you to make a number of small modifications in the way you eat, they will pay huge dividends in better health and extra brain power. If you don't have the time or energy to make any real changes in the way you eat, you can at the very least take these three simple steps:

1. Eat wholewheat bread (not "brown", "granary", "country wheat", or any other healthy-sounding name) instead of white bread. It costs a little more per loaf but it's more filling, so you will need less.

2. Eat at least one piece of fresh fruit, one whole carrot, and a salad or green vegetable every day.

3. At least twice a week, eat a good, balanced, cooked meal – you'll find several suggestions in the Menus For Students, on page 47. If you're dependent on the college canteen, and you don't have a kitchen of your own, take advantage of the recipes in Grains and Pulses *(see pages 115–119)*, and Salads *(see pages 136–143)*, many of which don't need cooking. Gather your friends around, and make a real meal of it.

This may not seem like much of a change, but consider the following nutritional facts. If you were eating a typical Western diet, composed of milk, cheese, beef, fish, eggs, margarine, white bread, cornflakes, sprouts, carrots, peas, salt, tea, apples, sugar, and potatoes – pretty fair by most nutritional standards – then some simple changes can make huge differences. Replace white bread with wholewheat bread, cornflakes with a wholewheat cereal, and add a handful of peanuts, some beans, potatoes, and apples to your diet to make up for the calories supplied by the sugar. Here's how your diet will improve as a result: you'll get 50 per cent more fibre, about 40 per cent more iron, 60 per cent more selenium, 54 per cent more folic acid (a B vitamin), 45 per cent more vitamin E, 38 per cent more vitamin B6, and equally significant extra quantities of choline, chromium, magnesium, zinc, and other vital nutrients. Extra amounts of these nutrients boost your resistance, give you more energy, aid concentration, and even help you burn the candle at both ends (as long as you don't do this too often).

As a student, you are likely to suffer from the same health problems as teenagers *(see page 41)*, but your worst enemy is likely to be exhaustion. Some of it is self-induced by too many late-night sessions putting the world to rights, or catching up on course work. Much of it is caused by the competitive pressures of university life today, and the strength-sapping stress of just keeping your head above water. The problem is aggravated by inadequate nutrition. The dramatic increase in student suicides in recent years, however, must be the most distressing fact of academic life today. Couple this with the rising dropout rate, and one is forced to search for underlying causes. Do students have to work harder than they used to? Are they under more pressure? Is university life too competitive? Perhaps, but one of the major reasons why many students fail to cope with what should be one of the most exciting and rewarding periods of their lives is a deficiency in many vital nutrients. Educational experts will consider this a simplistic theory. Consider, however, the B vitamins, for example. Wholegrain wheat is one of the best sources of these vitamins, which carry out a wide range of functions in the human body, and are particularly vital to the health of the nervous system. At periods of growth, our need for them is higher than at other times. When wheat is refined to white flour, the levels of the B vitamins fall sharply. Half the B2 (riboflavin) in wholewheat flour, nearly three-quarters of the B6 (pyridoxine), half the pantothenic acid, a quarter of the folic acid, and significant amounts of thiamin are lost in the refining process.

THE IMPORTANCE OF B VITAMINS

Lethargy, fatigue, weakness, and mood swings are classic symptoms of deficiency in many of the B vitamins. The shortfall in thiamin may be particularly important, since it is needed for carbohydrate metabolism. In the view of a nutritional medicine expert, those who consume a lot of refined carbohydrates, or junk food are particularly at risk from thiamin deficiency. Thiamin is vital to the normal function of the nervous system, and is essential for growth, and the sustaining of life itself. In the absence of thiamin, the body (and the brain in particular) is unable to obtain the energy it needs from food. In the 1940s, in one of the earliest nutritional experiments ever carried out, the effect of thiamin deficiency was studied in volunteers eating a diet that, in all other respects, was certainly superior to that eaten by most students today. Within days, the results were already dramatic. The volunteers began to suffer from sleeplessness, depression, irritability, difficulty in concentrating, inefficiency, forgetfulness, and fatigue. As time went on, certain more severe physical symptoms developed – shortness of breath, anaemia, and low blood pressure. Some of the volunteers even became suicidal.

In the Western world, the most severe problems caused by thiamin deficiency are seen in heavy drinkers. However, the depression, fatigue, and inability to concentrate, endemic to large sections of the student population have been noted over and over again as symptoms of nutritional deficiency. These problems are not all in the mind. It is unnecessary that so many of the high-potential youth of a generation should be afflicted by such problems, when good, basic foods can supply all that they need of the key nutrients. Be sure to include in your diet plenty of the Superfoods listed here, and give yourself a chance to make the most of your student years.

SUPERFOODS
FOR STUDENTS

Apples Apples are packed with vitamin C and fibre. Eat one every day for their natural goodness.

Brown rice A rich source of B vitamins, essential for the functioning of the nerves and brain, brown rice also provides energy for physical activity, minerals, and fibre.

Carrots are one of the great Superfoods. They contain beta-carotene, an antioxidant which protects the body from infection, and helps to maintain a clear skin.

Dried fruits A useful supply of energy, dried fruits, such as apricots, currants, figs, prunes, and raisins are also rich in minerals.

Eggs are the perfect convenience food – cheap, easy to cook, portable in hard-boiled form, and an excellent source of iron.

Nuts All varieties of nuts are densely packed with nourishment. Brazil nuts are especially good, since they are rich in thiamin and magnesium. Eat nuts freshly shelled whenever possible, and not too salted.

Sardines Because of the essential fatty acids and zinc they supply for brain function, sardines are a food for the intellect. Eat the soft bones in canned sardines for their plentiful supply of calcium.

Wholewheat bread Like brown rice, this is a rich source of B vitamins, minerals, and fibre.

MENUS
FOR STUDENTS

MONDAY
Bibi's Crab, Bacon, and Cheese Salad (p.138).
Crusty wholewheat roll.
Orange.

TUESDAY
Prawn and Tomato Curry (p.91).
Brown rice.
Green salad.
Yogurt with nuts and honey.

WEDNESDAY
Bean Casserole (p.116).
Spinach and Yogurt (p.130).
Toffee Bananas (p.157).

THURSDAY
Grilled Paprika Chicken (p.103).
New potatoes.
Broccoli with Garlic and Chilli (p.132).
Bunch of grapes.

FRIDAY
Scrambled Eggs with Smoked Mackerel (p.148).
Wholewheat toast.
Green salad with sliced avocado and toasted sunflower seeds.
Pear.

SATURDAY
Pasta with Tuna and Black Olive Sauce (p.121).
Wholewheat roll.
Watercress and iceberg lettuce salad.
Greek yogurt with fresh strawberries.

SUNDAY
Presia's Turkey Stir-Fry (p.108).
Peas and Lettuce (p.133).
Mixed green salad.
Apple.

YOUNG SINGLES

"I never thought I'd miss mum's cooking, but eating four Chinese take-aways in a row is definitely boring."

You're on your own now, and your life is what you make it. You're already settled into a job; you've left home for a place of your own; you have your own friends and social life. This is the age of romance, when the new love of your life can swallow up most of your time and attention. It can also be the age of broken hearts, and getting to grips with domestic chores and a job. Consequently, your diet should be supplying handsome insurance against stress of every kind – trials at work, romance gone awry, too many late nights. Turn to our simple rules for good eating on page 20, copy them out, pin them up in the first kitchen you can call your own, and stick to them.

Bedsitter cooking can degenerate into endless snacks of bread, cheese, and canned soup. Make sure you don't run out of the basics, like potatoes, carrots, onions, a good olive oil, lemons, sliced whole-wheat bread, and garlic. Stock up on salads – celery, red and yellow peppers, watercress, parsley, and spring onions – that will last for two or three days in the refrigerator. Also keep supplies of eggs, Greek yogurt, cottage cheese, milk, nuts, and seeds in the refrigerator. Have a bowl of mixed fruit handy. In the store cupboard, keep cans of tuna, cans of sardines in olive oil, tomatoes, sugar-free baked beans, and packets of brown rice, pasta, and dried herbs. With these stocks you'll always be able to whip up a healthy square meal – soup, salad, pasta, or risotto – no matter how rushed you are.

Cooking should be a pleasure as well as a necessity, and it can be a wonderful way to unwind at the end of a stressful day. Master a few basic survival recipes, so that you can rustle up a decent meal, such as a good, rich vegetable soup with beans, pasta, brown rice, or potatoes. Eat this with a chunk of wholewheat bread and a piece of fruit, and you have a nourishing, filling, very cheap meal. If it's a candlelit dinner for two you're preparing, you'll find some marvellous ideas for Superfast Food dishes in the Recipes *(see pages 78–164)*. Add some petits pois, an exotic sorbet, and fresh strawberries to the menu, and your guest will think you're a cordon bleu chef.

Learn to comb the vegetable stalls in your local market late on Saturday afternoon, when vegetables and salads are to be found at bargain prices. Teach yourself how to use nature's seasonings instead of loads of salt and bottled sauces: herbs and spices can give new zest to stews, soups, meat, and fish dishes. When you cook a chicken, fill the cavity with half a peeled onion, two or three whole cloves of garlic, and a sprig of thyme or rosemary.

For those in their twenties, stress often results from too many late nights, hectic romantic involvements, financial worries, and work problems. You should eat lots of wholegrain cereals, such as brown rice, oats, and wholewheat bread to help you cope, because these foods supply plenty of vitamin B, a rich diet for the nerves, and give you extra stamina, in the shape of calcium, iron, and magnesium.

If tea or the jar of instant coffee are always at hand at home or in the office, learn to ration yourself. Too much tea or coffee can make you very nervous, without you realizing the cause. Excess caffeine will prevent your body from absorbing some of the good minerals you may be feeding it. For maximum uptake of minerals, eat fruit or fresh vitamin C-rich vegetables with your meals, and drink mineral water or herb tea as occasional substitutes for tea and coffee.

If you started smoking and drinking in your teens, get a grip on these habits now. Instead of reaching for the cigarettes, keep a packet of sunflower seeds in your desk drawer to nibble at: they're little powerhouses of good nutrition. It is now known that the safe quantity of alcohol that will not damage the liver is 21 units a week for men, and 14 for women – one unit is equivalent to half a pint of beer, one pub measure of spirits, or a mean glassful of wine. Don't be browbeaten into drinking for social reasons – mineral water is seen in the most chic restaurants. As an alternative to alcohol, try apple or pineapple juice with sparkling mineral water, or one of those terrific new vegetable juice cocktails, chilled and spiked with lemon, or a spritzer – white wine and sparkling mineral water.

When you are in your twenties, your appearance is vitally important. Skin problems such as acne can be even more agonizing than they were in your teens. Don't panic. Try to keep one day a week when you eat nothing but fruit or vegetables, to give your whole system a good clean out. High on the list should be avocadoes. Research in Israel has shown that they help reconstitute collagen, a protein that keeps skin young. Other vital skin-restoring foods are cauliflower, broccoli, cabbage, chlorophyll-rich spinach and watercress, and all brightly coloured fruit, especially peaches, nectarines, and apricots. They're loaded with beta-carotene, which is great for skin.

WEIGHT PROBLEMS

If you are overweight, you will also respond to a fruit and vegetable "fast". If your weight is a real problem, keep a food diary in which you write down every single thing you eat or drink for a week. You may be amazed by the amount of high-fat, high-sugar junk you're loading into your body each day. Switch to Superfast Foods, and don't let yourself get hungry. Make sure that you eat something, such as an apple, a few dates, or a banana, at least every three hours. This stops the wild fluctuations in blood sugar that lead you inevitably to the biscuits or chocolate. Above all, don't diet. There is overwhelming evidence that dieting is the surest way to nourish a weight problem. Never resort to very-low-calorie diets, unless under the instruction and supervision of your own family doctor. The same is true of slimming pills, diuretics, herbal "slimming patches", and special diet clinics where you pay over the odds for drugs your own doctor would refuse to prescribe for you. The only way to lose weight in the long run is to retrain your eating habits so that you learn to eat healthily, and enjoy good food without being paranoid about what it's doing to your waistline.

For women, menstrual problems can be a real drag at this age. Cramps, irritability and tension, bloating, or a fresh crop of spots are among the monthly trials that so many women seem to accept as their normal lot. Far from being inevitable, however, menstrual problems are as much an index of ill health as muddy skin or lank hair, and just as avoidable. Go slow on caffeine, alcohol, and saturated fats. Eat plenty of wholegrain cereals, fresh fruit and vegetables, and nuts and seeds, which supply the magnesium, B vitamins, vitamin E, and iron that will help resolve your problems. Bananas are the Superfood for you. Rich in vitamin B6, iron, and potassium, they will help your kidneys cope with water retention problems.

SUPERFOODS
FOR YOUNG SINGLES

Avocados are extremely nutritious, highly digestible, and wonderfully filling. They also contain substances that are protective of the skin.

Bananas One of nature's original Superfast Foods, bananas are high in potassium, which is good for the heart, and full of fibre.

Carrots help keep your skin unblemished, your hair glossy, and your eyes keen. They also enhance the body's natural resistance to infection – particularly coughs, colds, and other respiratory problems.

Cauliflower is another resistance-booster, and a wonderful Superfast Food – you don't even have to cook it. It is important for strong bones, and healthy hair and skin.

Sunflower seeds are packed with nutrients, including vitamins, minerals, unsaturated fats, and protein that make them the perfect healthy snack.

Tuna What would we do without it? This convenient, canned protein-rich snack contains certain fats that have a strongly protective action on the heart.

Watercress Green is the colour for go and vitality. Eat watercress in soups, salads, and sandwiches.

MENUS
FOR YOUNG SINGLES

MONDAY
Michael's Welsh Rarebit (p.147).
Spinach and Yogurt (p.130).
Sticks of celery with a piece of your favourite cheese and a bunch
of grapes.

TUESDAY
Onion Soup (p.83) with a crusty wholewheat roll.
Salad of half an avocado, lettuce, tomatoes, watercress, and toasted
sunflower seeds.
Pear.

WEDNESDAY
Scrambled Eggs with Smoked Mackerel (p.148).
Green salad with watercress.
Baked Apples (p.159) with Greek yogurt.

THURSDAY
Salade Niçoise with tuna (p.137).
Steamed cauliflower tossed in oil and garlic.
Sliced mango.

FRIDAY
Marinated Fish I (p.99) with Fennel Parmigiana (p.128).
Rye crispbread with goat's cheese, a stick of celery, and radishes.
Peach.

SATURDAY
Pasta with Broccoli (p.124).
Grated carrot salad with watercress.
Greek yogurt with a spoonful of chopped nuts and a little honey.

SUNDAY
Chicken Jalfrezi (p.106).
Salad of grated carrots, almonds, and raisins, with mayonnaise dressing.
Compote of dried fruits.

THE SINGLE PARENT

"They've just launched the new sales campaign, I've got to go to the parents' meeting at Sally's school tonight, I haven't had a moment to do the shopping, and the child minder has just phoned to say she thinks Tim is coming down with chickenpox."

For most single parents, life seems to stagger from one crisis to another. Unlike the nuclear family, where burdens can be shared, in the one-parent family all the load falls on one pair of shoulders, and sometimes it takes all your strength and energy just to keep the support network going. Getting the children to school, keeping the home clean, doing the shopping, organizing meals, coping with officialdom, dealing with domestic emergencies, like a burst pipe or a broken fridge, keeping the children occupied during the school holidays – the list is endless. It can be an emotional, as well as a physical drain on your meagre reserves of stamina and health. You know you haven't got time to be ill, so you push yourself to the limits of your endurance, and beyond. You can't have a day in bed when you get a cold. You can't take the week off if you get flu, and your greatest dread is of being seriously ill, when the whole fragile house of cards might collapse around you.

Don't despair. Superfast Foods won't solve all your problems, but they will supply you with the best nutritional value for the least expense of effort, time, and money. Eat foods that nurture your resistance, your health, and your spirits. You cannot afford to eat badly. You cannot afford the "Vitality Robbers" in your kitchen – sweetened fizzy drinks; overprocessed, overpackaged, overpriced convenience foods; chemical apologies for yogurt; fishfingers with hardly any fish in them; cheap, frozen burgers, which are mostly rusk, gristle, and fat; breakfast cereals that are largely bran and sugar; the snacks that the children demand, brainwashed by television advertising; and the latest sweet-tooth craze – popular brands of chocolate bars, packaged as ice creams and drinks. Such foods supply many empty calories because they are high in fat, sugar, or salt, but low in the wonderful natural goodness of ordinary fresh food that you need to keep you and your family healthy. If you are on a tight budget, these convenience foods are the poorest kind of nutritional value for money.

For the single parent, life is tough enough without having to produce three different meals at three different times. Try making your own soups. They are quick and easy to prepare, and after you've tried out one or two you'll be making up your own as you go along. A bowl of

Leek and Potato Soup *(see page 80)*, or White Bean Soup with Garlic and Parsley *(see page 81)*, served with a crusty wholewheat roll and salad, is a satisfying meal in itself. If you eat roast chicken, make a stock with the carcass. Just throw it in a pan with a sliced onion, a carrot, and a bayleaf, and simmer for an hour or two. You can use it as the basis for a thick, rich soup later in the week.

Too many children – not to mention their parents – leave home in the morning with little more than a cup of tea inside them, and maybe a chocolate bar from the corner shop on their way to the bus stop. Pack your lot off with some ribsticking porridge, or good muesli, or at least a couple of slices of toast. Always make this with wholewheat bread. Turn to the table on page 22, compare the nutritional values of white and wholewheat bread, and vow you'll never buy another loaf of white sliced pap. Try to find a local baker who makes real wholewheat bread. It will cost a little more than white bread, but it's so much more solid and satisfying that you will eat less of it. If the children make a fuss, try giving them sandwiches made with one slice each of white and wholewheat bread, and put the white on top. You'll soon convert them.

You and your children may well enjoy a fast-food treat once in a while – not least because it gives you a break. It is what you eat most of the time, however, that matters. The occasional fish and chips, or burgers and French fries, or Chinese take-away should be just that: occasional treats. The rest of the time, serve up Superfast Foods for most of your family meals. There are dozens of dishes in the Recipes that will form the basis of a good, sit-down meal for all of you, and plenty of simple snacks that the children will enjoy, and that you can rustle up in a few minutes.

Children who don't learn the basics of cookery at home may grow up without the faintest idea of how to choose, prepare, and cook their own meals when the time comes. For their sake as much as your own, involve the children in the preparation of the meal – even if it only means laying the table at first. Get them to help you clean and prepare the vegetables, wash the salads, and grate the cheese. Then teach them how to make one or two simple dishes on their own that you can all enjoy together. When cooking becomes a family affair like this, it is instructive for the children, a help to you, and highly enjoyable all round. The sooner you introduce children to the idea that food and eating are an important part of life, and not just something you cram into a few minutes when the mood takes you, the better for everyone.

EATING FOR HEALTH

The health problems that you are probably most familiar with are stress and fatigue. How you eat can make a huge difference to your health. Oats, broccoli, chickpeas, canned fish, apples, brown rice, sesame seeds, and wholewheat bread are all Superfast Foods that will nourish your nervous system and enhance your energy. Get most of your protein from chicken or fish rather than red meat, because these are not only lower in fat, but also take less time to cook than red meat, and they are often cheaper.

If you are the sort of person who gets one cold after another that eventually turn into a sore throat, a hacking cough, and even bronchitis, then your resistance is much too low. Eat fresh fruit and fresh vegetables as often as you can for the wonderful vitality they impart. Especially good for boosting your defences are carrots, spinach, watercress, pumpkin, and mangoes. These are all wonderful sources of beta-carotene, converted by the body into vitamin A, which helps protect against infection.

Brewer's yeast – although strictly speaking a food supplement, rather than a Superfood – increases your intake of protein, zinc, iron, and magnesium, among other vital minerals, and it is spectacularly rich in B vitamins. You'll find brewer's yeast in chemists and health food shops. If you're feeling run-down, try making a quick energy-boosting drink with an added spoonful of brewer's yeast *(see pages 161–164)*.

SUPERFOODS
FOR THE SINGLE PARENT

Apples are the perfect, healthy snack for packed lunches and odd times when you feel hungry, and are popular in family puddings.

Apricots Fresh apricots can be found quite cheaply during the summer. Enjoy them while you can for their high levels of beta-carotene.

Broccoli is a food for building up your resistance; its dark green colour is an indication of its goodness.

Brown rice A great food for providing energy and nourishment, quick-cook brown rice has the advantage that it can also be prepared quickly.

Carrots Bursting with beta-carotene, carrots are among nature's greatest – and cheapest – protective Superfoods.

Chickpeas are rich in fibre, iron, and magnesium – three nutrients that you can't have too much of.

Eggs are the classic Superfast Food, and the basis of dozens of deliciously simple meals. Don't believe scaremongers who tell you on no account to eat more than two a week.

Onions Eat plenty of onions in winter, when your resistance is low, since they help protect you against coughs, colds, and flu.

Sesame seeds are a valuable source of many minerals, including iron and zinc.

MENUS
FOR THE SINGLE PARENT

MONDAY
Odds and Ends Eggs (p.86).
Mixed salad with lettuce, tomatoes, spring onions, and watercress.
Baked apples with plain yogurt.

TUESDAY
Bulgur Risotto (p.115).
Stewed carrots with butter and plenty of chopped fresh parsley.
Cheddar cheese with oatcakes and sticks of celery.
Apple.

WEDNESDAY
Potato Galette (p.126) with broccoli.
Grated carrot salad with raisins in a creamy mayonnaise dressing.
Ripe pears.

THURSDAY
Eggs in Onion Sauce (p.84).
Spinach purée.
Bread and Tomato Salad (p.137).
Fruit Crumble (p.159).

FRIDAY
Fish with Mushrooms (p.96).
Superfast Cabbage (p.125).
Quick-cook brown rice.
Stewed apricots with plain yogurt.

SATURDAY
Hearty Irish Stew (p.114).
Steamed cauliflower tossed in butter with plenty of parsley.
Bunch of grapes.

SUNDAY
Chicken with Garlic (p.104).
Turnip and Potato Cream (p.127).
French beans.
Fresh fruit salad with orange juice.

THE SUPERWOMAN

"He's away on a golfing weekend with the managing director, and I'm left to cope with the kids and the shopping, and there's an advertising shoot on Sunday that I've got to supervise."

If you are a modern wife and mother, and you have a job, then you may not be staring poverty in the face, or living in appalling conditions, but your situation still has its own unique stresses. The job gets tougher as you climb the promotion ladder. You are chronically short of time, and what little you have to spare is probably devoted to your husband and children – and if you thought toddlers were a handful, just wait until your children head for the teens, when you'll find they need even more of your time and attention. Domestic pressures accumulate to create further demands on your time and attention: cooking dinner parties, organizing birthdays, and attending parent evenings at the children's school. Sometimes you really wish you were "Superwoman".

Good food is not always your top priority, and mealtimes are often scrappy affairs – a quick raid on the freezer for fishfingers and oven chips, or ready-made burgers, complete with buns and sauce from the supermarket. Avoid such temptations as lunching off a chocolate bar and a coffee, or serving up endless, microwaved, television dinners because you feel tired to death, and it's too much trouble to cook. Don't turn to sweet snacks for an instant energy lift that will let you down later, as well as aggravating any weight problems you may have.

For these rich, demanding years of your life, only first-class nourishment is good enough: you can't be a "Superwoman" on anything but Superfood. Whole grains, fresh fruit and vegetables, chicken, fish, raw salads, fresh herbs to grow in pots on the windowsill, yogurt, milk, cheese, supplies of fresh nuts – preferably still in their shells – and seeds should all be basics on your shopping list. If daily shopping is out of the question, choose vegetables, like potatoes, carrots, and onions, which will stay fresh happily for a few days, stored in a cool place, out of the light, in brown paper bags. In the refrigerator, keep supplies of salads, such as sweet peppers, celery, fennel, and watercress.

INCREASE YOUR INTAKE OF MINERALS

A survey of the eating habits of adults, carried out recently in Australia, showed that 85 per cent of women consumed less than the recommended level of zinc, and 39 per cent of women less than the recommended level of magnesium. The diets of men, incidentally, were similarly deficient, with 67 per cent of men consuming below the recommended level of zinc, and 50 per cent below that of magnesium. If your body is short of zinc, it will show up in fertility problems of all kinds – miscarriages and infertility for women, a low sperm count for men – and in poor hair and skin. Since zinc is also vital for your immune defences, you'll be an easy victim for passing infections – colds, influenza, sore throats, and bronchitis – something that you certainly can't afford. Good sources of zinc are shellfish of all kinds, beef, lamb, shrimps, crab meat, sardines, cheese, and eggs.

Even simple changes in your diet can make a world of difference. When a women's magazine persuaded a number of its readers to join an experiment that involved eating fewer processed foods, less sugar, and more fresh fruit and vegetables, the volunteers – young and old – were astounded by how much better they felt.

Magnesium deficiency is often responsible for what has been dubbed the Tired Housewife Syndrome. Green vegetables, nuts and seeds, wholewheat flour, brown rice, and seafood are all good sources of magnesium. If you eat none of these foods, don't be surprised if you often feel too tired to get your act together. You may be surprised to learn, however, that the supposedly healthy bran cereal you sometimes eat for breakfast can, in fact, bind magnesium, zinc, and calcium, and carry them straight out of your body.

The quick coffee pick-me-up can be disastrous for women who are already stressed and overworked. One reason for this is that if you drink coffee at meals that contain protein, some of the minerals in that protein, including iron, will not be absorbed by your body. Green vegetables and salads, and fruit, eaten at the same meal, however, will actually enhance the body's absorption of iron. Even if you are well above the level at which you can be considered clinically anaemic, a shortfall of iron in your diet can drain your energies and spirits.

During these years of ever-growing responsibility – husband, children, and career – the stress and the pressure never let up. At these times, you need the nerve-proofing supplied by foods rich in B vitamins. Oats are particularly good for you – a wonderful, nourishing food for the whole nervous system. Also eat wholewheat bread and brown rice for vitamin B.

Stress and tension are bad news for your heart, and although it might seem early days to start worrying, make sure that your diet supplies plenty of the antioxidant vitamins, A and C, and beta-carotene, which are all found in brightly coloured fruit and vegetables. Eat oily fish, like sardines, mackerel, and salmon. The oils in these fish have a protective effect on the heart. Use extra-virgin olive oil in salads. Eat plenty of onions and as much garlic as you can.

What is good for your heart and nervous system is also good for your skin – always a faithful mirror of how well, or badly, you are eating. Carrots, broccoli, melon, spinach, nectarines, apricots, and kiwi fruit will do more to put the bloom back in your skin than any designer face cream. So will the chlorophyll and other compounds in green leafy vegetables, and the vitamin E and oils in seeds, nuts, and avocados.

You are probably aware that milk and cheese are rich in calcium, and that if you don't get plenty of calcium in your food, you are likely to develop osteoporosis later on. What you may not know, however, is that calcium isn't the whole story. Without enough magnesium, your body may not be able to absorb the calcium. Furthermore, if you're low in vitamin D – the nutrient produced by skin on exposure to sunlight – you could still be at risk from osteoporosis. In addition, you may not know that milk is by no means the best source of calcium. An average helping of canned sardines – as long as you eat the little bones – will supply nearly twice as much calcium as 300 ml (½ pt) of milk. Nuts, seeds, and green vegetables are other good sources of calcium, while tofu – made from soybeans – is richer in calcium than any other known food. Try it in a stir-fry, with plenty of green vegetables and nuts.

One of the great bonuses of a healthy diet is that menstrual problems, like cramps, irritability, bloating, and general malaise can gradually diminish. In a number of studies, premenstrual syndrome has been conclusively linked with diets poor in vital nutrients, and high in saturated fats from meat, cheese and butter, refined sugars, additives such as artificial flavourings, food colourings, sweeteners, and coffee.

SUPERFOODS
FOR THE SUPERWOMAN

Almonds are a very concentrated food, rich in protein, fats, zinc, magnesium, potassium, iron, and some B vitamins.

Cabbage is good for your skin and your heart, and enhances your resistance to disease.

Grapes are uniquely nourishing and fortifying. When they are in season, buy a big bunch for the family dessert.

Low-fat cheese Feta cheese, cottage cheese, and ricotta are all good sources of protein and calcium. Eat them in a salad for a quick, delicious meal in itself – ideal for a weekend lunch.

Melons Cantaloupe and Ogen melons are rich sources of beta-carotene. Wonderful for cleansing the body of impurities, melons are best eaten either on their own, or at the start of a meal for the sake of your digestion.

Oats Food for the nerves, oats are a prime source of vitamin B, iron, and zinc.

Sardines These are every woman's friend. A highly nutritious food, sardines are rich in protein, vitamins D and B12, calcium, iron, and zinc. This means that they are great for your bones, heart, and circulatory system.

MENUS
FOR THE SUPERWOMAN

MONDAY
Eggs Mornay (p.87).
Cabbage with Onion and Bacon (p.125).
Mixed green salad.
Compote of mixed dried fruit with low-fat *fromage frais*.

TUESDAY
Prawn, Broccoli, and Leek Stir-fry (p.90).
Quick-cook brown rice.
Baked Apples (p.159).

WEDNESDAY
Beef Stir-fry (p.101).
Quick Mashed Potatoes (p.127).
Spinach Italian-Style (p.129).
Fruit Crumble with apples and blackberries (p.159).

THURSDAY
Pasta with Salmon, Mushroom, and Cream Sauce (p.120).
Green salad with watercress and toasted sunflower seeds.
Bunch of grapes.

FRIDAY
Sweetcorn and Haddock Chowder (p.78).
Wholewheat rolls.
Mixed green salad with tomatoes and chopped green herbs.
Goat's cheese.
Fresh peaches.

SATURDAY
Lamb and Pine Kernel Koftas (p.102), with wholewheat pita bread.
Green salad of lettuce, rocket, watercress, and parsley.
Raspberries, blackcurrants, and cream.

SUNDAY
Mediterranean Chicken (p.111).
Baked potatoes or boiled new potatoes.
Cauliflower with Garlic and Chilli (p.132).
Fresh fruit.

THE PROFESSIONAL COUPLE

He gets home from the weekly office conference to find a message on the answering machine: "Hello darling! I'm still in the meeting, but I'm aiming for the 7.30, and should be home at around 9 pm. Do you mind organizing dinner?"

Two busy lives, two demanding careers, and no children. Work forces have been pared to the bone, competition is fiercer than ever, and the pressures to perform at consistently high levels are relentless. You may live with the constant spectre of redundancy. Your life often involves travelling on tight schedules, rushing from an airport to an appointment, a disturbed night in a hotel bedroom, then back to the airport, and straight to another city. You are often surviving on airline food, sandwiches sent into the boardroom, and rushed breakfasts. This lifestyle can play havoc with your digestive system, create enormous stress, and cause backache, neck ache, and headache.

You probably both think you're pretty fit and healthy – it has been years, after all, since either of you took a day off due to sickness. You get regular exercise, and you have two good holidays a year. Maybe you are just papering over the cracks, however, and getting by on lots of stimulants, like coffee, alcohol, ginseng, and guarana, while your natural resilience carries you through.

You are both slightly obsessed with your weight and your looks. You're likely to follow the very latest in dieting fashions. It is also quite possible that you exercise too much. The combination of these two factors, aggravated by your erratic eating habits, could easily leave you on the nutritional borderline. You are burning up your reserves, and there is little or nothing left for emergencies. This may surprise and shock you. After all, you believe that you eat a healthy diet by most standards. From a health point of view, however, this is a crucial time for both men and women. The health habits – good or bad – that you are establishing now will determine just how fit and active you are in ten, twenty, or fifty years from now.

You need masses of the antioxidant vitamins, A, C, and E, and beta-carotene. These are vital, since it is now known that they provide protection against many forms of cancer, heart disease, and infections. They also keep you young – quite literally – because they work against the ageing process, both internally and externally, where they help keep skin supple, elastic, and free of wrinkles. Your diet must also supply lavish amounts of B vitamins from foods such as wholewheat bread, oats, and chicken – essential for coping with the intense pressures on your nervous system. Minerals, particularly iron and magnesium, will help protect you against fatigue. Women especially should be eating foods rich in all the minerals – not just calcium – to protect their bones long past the menopause, and to reduce the likelihood of chronic iron deficiency. Be sure that your diet contains plenty of fibre. The fibre naturally present in fruit, oats, brown rice, wholemeal bread, beans, and vegetables is the sort you need, rather than bran, which combines with calcium, magnesium, iron, and zinc to carry them out of your body.

Caffeine and tannin can also block your mineral uptake. If you drink a cup of tea or coffee with your boiled eggs you will absorb little of the valuable iron in the egg yolk. Drink a glass of orange juice instead – the vitamin C it contains will actively promote the absorption of iron. A glass of good red wine a day may help protect you from heart attacks, but a bottle a day will not only increase your risk of heart disease, but also destroy stores of your vitamin B. The same is true of all alcohol.

No doubt your bathroom cabinets are stuffed with state-of-the-art vitamin and mineral supplements, including high-dose antioxidants. But vitamins and minerals, we must never forget, are not the whole nutritional story. It is important that you eat whole fresh foodstuffs for the myriad other health-enhancing substances present in them. By all means take vitamin supplements, but make sure that your diet is based the fresh Superfoods you're lucky enough to be able to afford.

COOK YOUR OWN FRESH FOOD

Although money is not a problem for you, the demands of both your jobs leave you with little time or energy for cooking. Frequently, dinner consists of expensive ready-made meals, usually thrown into the microwave, and eaten with a bottle of decent wine. That microwaved dinner may be expensive and it may taste delicious. On the other hand, have you ever thought about its nutritional content? The protein value of meat, fish, or poultry is not destroyed by cooking, but other nutrients are vulnerable to heat, particularly vitamin C and some of the B vitamins.

Food that has been harvested, transported, prepared, cooked, chilled, transported again, quite often frozen at this stage, and then cooked again will not have the same natural goodness or nutritional value as the original fresh produce. Get into the habit of preparing meals with fresh ingredients. This doesn't mean spending hours in the kitchen. Leaf through the recipes included in the Menus for the Professional Couple, opposite, and you'll find dozens of simple, delicious dishes, some of which can be ready in as little as five minutes. Dinner parties can be home-cooked with Superfast Foods – a pleasant change from the eternal smoked salmon, followed by a pricey cook-chill dish, and ice cream or cheese.

You may think of preparing and cooking meals as yet another demand on your precious time. Consider it, instead, as one of the most satisfying and creative hobbies we know. If your kitchen is starkly functional, change the décor, and make it a friendlier place to be in, with plants and pictures, or music. Use the time in your kitchen as relaxation therapy, to help unwind the mind while it nurtures the body.

SUPERFOODS
FOR THE PROFESSIONAL COUPLE

Avocados are delicious and nourishing, rich in potassium to help counter fatigue, and well-endowed with antioxidant vitamins.

Extra-virgin olive oil is the best, not only for flavour but also for its beneficial effects on the digestion and circulatory systems.

Goat's cheese Enjoy this increasingly popular dairy product because it is low in calories, easily digested, and a good source of many of the vital B vitamins.

Greek yogurt Use it instead of cream with puddings. Although it seems rich, it is still much lower in fat than single cream – 10 per cent as opposed to 21 per cent – and a lot more digestible.

Red, green, and yellow vegetables Sweet peppers, carrots, green and red cabbage, beetroot, spinach, radishes, and broccoli are wonderful natural foods, and high in antioxidants.

Shellfish Oysters, scallops, crab, lobster, prawns, and shrimps contain a wealth of essential minerals, including magnesium, zinc, and iodine.

Sun-dried tomatoes are a lovely way to put some sunshine on the menu – even in winter. Use them to enhance the flavour and colour of many dishes.

Whole grains life in the fast lane needs the four-star nutrition of wholewheat bread and brown rice, rich in B vitamins. Millet and buckwheat are other good grains to consider.

MENUS
FOR THE PROFESSIONAL COUPLE

MONDAY
Lamb cutlets brushed with olive oil, and grilled on a bed of rosemary.
Bulgur with Aubergines, Almonds, and Raisins (p.115).
Mixed green salad.
Pears.

TUESDAY
Italian Pan-fried Liver (p.101).
Broccoli tossed in olive oil and lemon juice.
Oatcakes with goat's cheese and grapes.

WEDNESDAY
Red and Yellow Eggs (p.89).
Spinach and Yogurt (p.130).
Salad of lettuce and rocket.
Selection of cheeses.
Apples.

THURSDAY
Devilled Sardines (p.98).
Wholewheat pita bread.
Avocado and watercress salad with pine nuts.
Compote of dried fruit with Greek yogurt.

FRIDAY
Fish Steaks with a Sesame Seed Coating on a Bed of
Warm Spinach (p.92).
Bread and Tomato Salad (p.137).
Fresh strawberries.

SATURDAY
Crudités – carrots, beetroot, and cucumber –
served with French Dressing (p.143).
Spiced Indian Chicken (p.112).
Brown rice served with olive oil and a little garlic.
Orange Mango Fool (p.160).

SUNDAY
Duck Breasts with Green Pepper Sauce (p.107).
Italian Vegetable Grill (p.134).
Green salad with a piece of Brie.
Peaches.

MIDDLE-AGED FREEDOM

"The children are both married, the mortgage is paid up, and we've got nothing to worry about. I should be happy, but I've spent 25 years cooking three meals a day, most days of the week, most weeks in the year, and I'm bored to death with it. I wouldn't care if we lived the rest of our lives on convenience foods."

A certain amount of role reversal is common in one's fifties. More and more men take early retirement, and often discover the joys of cooking. The women, free at last of domestic responsibilities, often return to a job that they enjoy, or spend new-found time on hobbies and leisure pursuits. Many retired people wonder how they ever found the time to go to work. Probably the last thing either of you wants right now is to spend hours in the kitchen. At this time of life, however, good nutrition is just as important as at any other stage in human development, and eating well now could save you from many of the miseries of old age, and guarantee you a long, healthy, and active retirement.

Heart disease, cancer, arthritis, rheumatism, cataracts, and wrinkles are all assumed to be part of the price we pay for living longer. Many recent, exciting studies have shown that these manifestations of the ageing process are, in fact, the result of cell damage caused by free radicals, which are by-products of the body's chemical activity. A high intake of fresh vegetables and fruit, which are rich in the antioxidant vitamins, A, C, and E, and beta-carotene, can protect joints, heart, arteries, and skin from much of the ravage of the years.

VITAMIN C AND CANCER

There have been massive amounts of research over the past few years into one of the antioxidants, vitamin C. The School of Public Health at the University of California has undertaken such research into population studies. This research has revealed the consistently protective effect of a diet high in fruit and vegetables against many forms of cancer. The studies stress that people with a low intake of vitamin C run an increased risk of various cancers, including gastric, breast, lung, stomach, and cervical cancers. A number of American dietary surveys of vitamin C intake and absorption have demonstrated that substantial groups of people in the United States may be at a high risk of cancer because their intake of vitamin C is so low. A staggering 50 per cent of women in the United States were shown to have intakes below 55 mg a day – the recommended daily intake there is 60 mg – and from 10 to 30 per cent of men had levels below the recommended intake range. Many experts believe that, even with intakes of up to 88 mg of vitamin C a day, which is more than twice the daily recommended amount in Great Britain, people are still in increased health risk groups.

So whoever is in charge in the kitchen needs to make sure that they serve up plenty of the fresh fruit and vegetables that are rich in antioxidant vitamins. Eat a carrot a day – it is spectacularly high in beta-carotene. Red, yellow, and green peppers, spinach, blackcurrants, strawberries, and nuts are well supplied with antioxidants, as well as many other substances.

To help keep joints and skin youthful, you need the protective oils found in oily fish, such as salmon, mackerel, sardines, and tuna. They lose very little of their goodness, incidentally, when they are canned, and therefore make a perfect Superfast Food snack.

The woman of the house may be going through the menopause. This doesn't have to mean that all the horror stories will come true – hot flushes, weight gain, headaches, and brittle bones. A healthy woman, eating wisely and well, should sail through the menopause without undue problems. If you aren't so fortunate, seek expert advice. Make sure that your diet is high in spinach, wholewheat bread, onions, avocados, carrots, oats, and sesame seeds. Do not believe the pessimists who tell you that it is too late to do anything about your bones, once you have reached the menopause. You can still help yourself to better bones. A diet containing plenty of calcium, magnesium, zinc, and vitamin D will help. So look to your shopping basket, and make sure it is filled with green leafy vegetables, green, red, and yellow peppers, green and orange-yellow fruit, chickpeas, pumpkin seeds, sardines, yogurt, and low-fat cheese. Eat at least three of these foodstuffs each day.

Young women have a much lower risk of heart disease than young men, for whom it is the most common cause of premature death in the West. Once the menopause is reached, however, women are just as likely to suffer this scourge to the health, and should be aware how vital a role the diet can play. Make sure that your diet includes plenty of the antioxidant-rich foods, as mentioned above, plenty of fibre from wholegrain cereals and vegetables, essential fatty acids from oily fish, nuts, and seeds, and plenty of onions and garlic, which are good for the heart and circulation.

SUPERFOODS
FOR THE MIDDLE-AGED

Beetroot is traditionally a powerful tonic for building up those who are run down, and the convalescent.

Cabbage and other green leafy vegetables are good sources of beta-carotene and minerals, and great cleansers to the system.

Chickpeas Widely eaten in the Middle East, this wonderfully rich pulse has a high fibre content and lots of calories – ideal in a main dish.

Nectarines and Peaches Like all yellow-orange fruit, these are rich in beta-carotene, which will help protect you from the effects of ageing. The skins are a good source of fibre, so clean them thoroughly, but don't peel them.

Oats are a good source of easily digested protein, health-giving polyunsaturated fats, B vitamins, vitamin E, and an abundance of essential minerals. The fibre in oats helps reduce cholesterol levels, and so promotes healthy arteries.

Salmon, Sardines, and Tuna, among the most nutritious fish, are rich in protective oils. Choose them fresh and bright-eyed.

Sesame seeds are very rich in protein, iron, and zinc, and have a high level of polyunsaturated fatty acids, which are good for the heart. These little seeds are great for quelling fatigue, and in the Middle East, they are considered a sexual tonic.

Sweet peppers All sweet peppers are an excellent source of vitamin C, while the red and yellow ones also provide a good supply of vitamin A. They contain iron and potassium, which, thanks to their vitamin C content, are well absorbed by the body. They also have fibre, and are low in calories.

MENUS
FOR THE MIDDLE-AGED

MONDAY
Presia's Eggs Bolognese (p.84).
Steamed broccoli.
Celery and carrot sticks.
Peach or nectarine.

TUESDAY
Fish with Mushrooms (p.96).
Green leafy vegetables.
New potatoes.
Pears.

WEDNESDAY
Instant Chickpea Casserole (p.117).
Spinach and Yogurt (p.130).
Tomato salad.
Bunch of grapes.

THURSDAY
Courgette Pasta (p.123).
Iceberg lettuce, tomato, and watercress salad.
Oatcakes with a piece of your favourite cheese.

FRIDAY
Marinated Fish II (p.99).
Piquant Beetroot (p.135).
Avocado and watercress salad.
Baked apple with a little *crème fraîche*.

SATURDAY
Lamb Peperonata (p.103).
Quick-cook brown rice.
Mixed green salad with fresh green herbs.
Yogurt with a spoonful of blackcurrant purée.

SUNDAY
Chicken in Chablis (p.112).
French Green Beans with Tomatoes (p.130).
Chicory salad with lots of fresh parsley.
Sliced bananas with nuts and a little cream.

THE ELDERLY

"We're approaching our seventies, we're hale and hearty, but neither of us has tremendous appetites any more, and we do seem to have drifted into a bit of a rut when it comes to eating, sticking to the same food most of the time. Does it really matter though, at our age? Our parents didn't know anything about this nutrition business, and they were all right."

In an ideal world, Darby and Joan grow old together. In real life, sadly, there are more often widows and widowers. Either way, however, it is often the same story for the elderly: as appetites and energies dwindle, older people tend to succumb to random eating habits, with endless cups of tea and biscuits, snacks instead of proper meals, and bread and cheese to assuage the hunger pangs.

At 60 and over, although you certainly don't need the square meals of a 25-year-old, it is vital to make sure that your diet is rich in the nutrients you need to keep fit and in good shape. Poor digestion, stiff joints, failing memory, sight, and hearing, and heart problems are by no means inevitable just because you're in your sixties or seventies. They are symptoms of cell damage, which can be slowed down – if not averted – by a high intake of the antioxidant vitamins, A, C, and E. The Superfoods that supply lavish amounts of these, such as fresh fruit and vegetables, should feature in your daily diet, and garlic, extra-virgin olive oil, onions, and oily fish are all good news for ageing hearts.

Researchers who studied the eating habits of over 2,000 residents, aged 65 and over, in Adelaide, Australia, found that the nutrients most often poorly supplied by their diets were calcium, zinc, folic acid – one of the B vitamins – magnesium, and copper. What's more, fewer than 13 per cent of those questioned were getting enough fibre in their diet. It is hardly a coincidence that all of these nutrients are richly supplied in wholewheat bread, but grossly depleted in refined white flour. Wholewheat flour supplies more than twice as much calcium, zinc, and folic acid, seven times more magnesium, twice as much copper, nearly twice as much iron, and nearly three times as much fibre as white flour. Wholewheat flour contains more protein than white, and it is a good source of B vitamins, which are essential for the brain and nervous system, and which also keep your spirits buoyant. Wholewheat flour also contains vitamin E, the antioxidant which is precious for your heart and arteries. Barely a trace of vitamin E remains in white flour. If you want to be a sprightly octogenarian, opt for wholewheat bread, and if a cup of tea without a biscuit is unthinkable, buy wholewheat biscuits.

EAT EASILY DIGESTED FOODS

When you are in your sixties, you should enjoy foods that supply the most nutrients in the most digestible form. You are not just what you eat: you are what your body can absorb from what you eat. Protect your digestive system with a diet rich in fibre, supplied by plant foodstuffs – an apple a day is a preferable source of this fibre than extra bran, which can prevent the body from absorbing vital minerals. The Adelaide survey studied the nutritional supplements being taken regularly by the elderly, and found that one in four of the women, and more than one in five of the men, were taking supplementary bran that further diminished the amounts of calcium, magnesium, and zinc being absorbed from their food. Plain yogurt is especially good if you have problems digesting milk, as well as being a useful source of protein, calcium, and B vitamins. When they're in season, enjoy strawberries, raspberries, bilberries, and blackberries. These possess cleansing properties: they help flush out uric acid from the system, as do celery, cabbage, and leeks.

Important for brain function are the essential fatty acids found in oily fish, such as salmon, sardines, tuna, and anchovies. These are also good sources of zinc and iron, as well as great convenience foods in their canned form. These essential fatty acids will also do wonders for your joints. Eat plenty of dark green, leafy vegetables – the darker green, the better. They're crammed with goodness. Researchers are just beginning to explore these common foods, often with startling results. They are important sources of magnesium, deficiency of which can be responsible for insomnia, confusion, poor memory, apathy, poor appetite, constipation, and problems of cardiac rhythm. Don't these symptoms remind you of too many elderly people we all know? If you take diuretic drugs, remember that they wash out minerals, including magnesium, so you will need a regular, high intake of this mineral from green leafy vegetables.

You may not feel inclined to spend much time in the kitchen, but regular meals – however small – are vital for you. Try to make mealtimes special, even if you're on your own, because enjoying food is important for the digestion. Lay the table, put a sprig of flowers in a vase, eat slowly, and chew the food well. A good meal doesn't have to be cooked – a wholewheat roll, a piece of cheese, a stick of celery, and an apple make up a nourishing square meal, and in winter, you can flesh it out with a bowl of simple vegetable soup *(see pages 78–83).*

SUPERFOODS
FOR THE ELDERLY

Chicken is a low-fat, versatile source of protein, rich in B vitamins, zinc, and iron. Eat free-range chicken, if possible.

Chicory and Endive are both wonderful tonics for the liver and digestive system. If you find endive too tough as a raw salad, cook it as you would green leafy vegetables, combining it perhaps with spinach.

Dried fruit Rich in energy and fibre, dried peaches and apricots are also a good year-round source of beta-carotene.

Garlic and Onions will take care of your heart. Eat plenty of them, raw in salads, or in thick vegetable soups *(see pages 78–83)* or in simple stews.

Oats are a great protective food, rich in fibre, minerals, and protein. Eat them in porridge, or Muesli *(see page 152)*, for a comforting breakfast.

Strawberries are not only a delicious treat, but also a cleansing tonic with a mild laxative effect, and they possess useful minerals.

Wholewheat bread Far superior to white bread, this wonderful, natural foodstuff is full of nutrients.

MENUS
FOR THE ELDERLY

MONDAY
Oats and Broccoli Pottage (p.78) and a wholewheat roll.
Mixed green salad.
Goat's cheese.
Apple.

TUESDAY
Marinated Fish I (p.99).
Steamed broccoli.
Wholewheat roll.
Chicory salad with chopped, fresh parsley.
Ripe pear.

WEDNESDAY
Eggs in Onion Sauce (p.84).
Spinach purée.
Sticks of celery and carrot.
Apple.

THURSDAY
Braised Chicken (p.110).
Green leafy vegetables.
Quick Mashed Potatoes (p.127).
Peach and Apricot Compote (p.156).

FRIDAY
Salmon en Papillote (p.94).
Mixed green salad.
Strawberries with *crème fraîche.*

SATURDAY
Scrambled Eggs (p.147).
Puréed spinach with a little nutmeg.
A piece of farmhouse Cheddar cheese, with sticks of celery.

SUNDAY
Chicken with Thyme and Lemon (p.113).
Baked potato.
Mixed green salad with plenty of cress.
Lightly stewed raspberries and blackcurrants with Greek yogurt.

THE RECIPES

The information beside each recipe indicates how long the dish takes to prepare – and cook or marinate, where applicable – and how many people the dish serves.

Ingredients are listed with both metric and imperial measurements, either of which can be used, but the two systems should not be mixed.

SOUPS

SWEETCORN AND HADDOCK CHOWDER

This is a one-pot meal. Keep the cooking time short by cutting the potatoes small so that they cook through in 10 minutes. Ideally they should crumble and thicken the soup.

Preparation time

5 minutes

Cooking time

25 minutes

Serves 4

Heat the oil, and fry the bacon until crisp. Remove and reserve. Fry the onion until softened but not brown, add the bay leaf, thyme, potato, sweetcorn, milk, buttermilk, and water. Simmer for 10 minutes, add the fish and chives, and simmer gently for a further 5 minutes. Season to taste with salt and freshly ground black pepper, and serve with the strips of bacon arranged over the top.

INGREDIENTS

2 tbs sunflower oil
75 g/3 oz streaky bacon, cut into strips
1 onion, chopped
1 bay leaf
a sprig of fresh thyme
2 medium potatoes, peeled and diced
375 g/12 oz can of sweetcorn, drained
300 ml/½ pt milk
300 ml/½ pt buttermilk
150 ml/¼ pt water
250 g/8 oz undyed smoked haddock, cut into 2.5 cm/1 in cubes, skin and bones removed
1 tbs chives, chopped
salt and pepper

OATS AND BROCCOLI POTTAGE

Preparation time

10 minutes

Cooking time

15 minutes

Serves 4

Heat the oil and sweat the onions until they are soft. Add the broccoli, and stir for a couple of minutes. Add the oats, and stir for another minute or two. Slowly add the milk and stock or water, stirring. Cover and simmer very gently for 10 minutes. Season with a little freshly ground pepper and nutmeg. Just before serving the soup, stir in the cream and sprinkle with the chopped chives.

INGREDIENTS

1 tbs olive oil
6 spring onions, chopped
500 g/1 lb broccoli florets
50 g/2 oz porridge oats
1 litre/1¾ pt half and half milk and vegetable stock
freshly ground pepper
freshly ground nutmeg
1 tbs single cream
1 tbs chopped chives

CREAM OF PEA SOUP

INGREDIENTS

50 g/2 oz butter

4 spring onions, chopped

heart of 1 lettuce, shredded

500 g/1 lb fresh or frozen shelled peas

pepper

600 ml/1 pt water

1 tbs chopped fresh mint

2 tbs Greek strained yogurt

This soup makes an appealing dinner party starter, served with crisp crackers.

Melt the butter in a pan, and add the spring onions, lettuce, peas, and pepper to taste. Cover and cook gently for 5 minutes. Add the water and mint, bring gradually to the boil, then simmer for 7 minutes. Purée in a food processor or blender. Stir in the yogurt, and serve immediately with crusty wholemeal rolls and cheese.

Preparation time

5 minutes

Cooking time

20 minutes

Serves 4

WATERCRESS SOUP

INGREDIENTS

1 tbs olive oil

1 medium onion, peeled and finely chopped

2 cloves garlic, peeled and finely chopped

1 tsp curry powder

3 bunches of watercress, thoroughly washed, with stalks remaining

900 ml/1½ pt vegetable stock

salt and freshly ground black pepper

small carton of *fromage frais*

Heat the oil, sweat the onion until soft, add the garlic, and cook for 1 minute. Add the curry powder, and cook for another minute, stirring vigorously. Turn down the heat, add the watercress, and stir for 2 minutes until it wilts. Add the stock, season with salt and pepper to taste, and simmer for 10 minutes. Liquidize, and serve hot with a swirl of *fromage frais* in each dish. Alternatively, this soup is delicious served chilled as a summer starter.

Preparation time

5 minutes

Cooking time

15 minutes

Serves 4

LEEK AND CHEESE SOUP

Preparation time

5 minutes

Cooking time

25 minutes

Serves 4

Wash, trim, and finely slice the leeks. Heat the butter, and sauté the leeks until they are soft. Stir in the flour, and cook for a couple of minutes. Add the chicken stock and milk. Cover, and simmer for about 15 minutes, then put in a blender or food processor, and blend until smooth. Add the cheese, and heat until it has melted. Stir in the dill, season with salt and pepper, and serve.

INGREDIENTS
500 g/1 lb leeks
25 g/1 oz butter
25 g/1 oz wholemeal flour
400 ml/scant ¾ pt chicken stock
300 ml/½ pt milk
75 g/3 oz soft cheese – perhaps Boursin with herbs – cut into small pieces
1 tbs fresh dill, finely chopped
salt and pepper

LEEK AND POTATO SOUP

Preparation time

10 minutes

Cooking time

30–35 minutes

Serves 4

Fry the potatoes, onion, leeks (reserve some of the leeks for a garnish), and garlic in the butter for 8–10 minutes. This should be done slowly so that the vegetables do not brown. Add the stock, and bring to the boil. Simmer gently until the vegetables are tender – about 20–25 minutes. Either sieve or liquidize. Return to a clean pan, and add the cream, pepper, and parsley. Stir over a gentle heat until hot. Sprinkle with strips of leek, and serve.

INGREDIENTS
375 g/12 oz potatoes, peeled and chopped
1 large onion, finely chopped
2 large leeks, cleaned and roughly chopped
1 clove garlic, crushed
50 g/2 oz butter
900 ml/1½ pt vegetable stock
150 ml/¼ pt double cream
pepper
2 tbs finely chopped fresh parsley

FRESH TOMATO SOUP

INGREDIENTS

1 medium onion, finely chopped
2 or 3 cloves garlic, chopped
3 tbs olive oil
750 g/1½ lb tomatoes, peeled and quartered
900 ml/1½ pt vegetable stock
2 or 3 thick slices of stale wholemeal bread with the crusts removed
salt and pepper
1 tbs ready-made pesto

Make this in summer when you can find beautifully ripe, red tomatoes that are full of flavour.

Sauté the onion and garlic in the olive oil. When they are translucent, add the tomatoes, and cook over a moderate heat until they melt. Add the vegetable stock, cook for 4 or 5 minutes, add the bread, coarsely crumbled, and cook another 2 or 3 minutes. Season with salt and pepper, and serve tepid with the pesto.

Preparation time

10 minutes

Cooking time

10 minutes

Serves 4

WHITE BEAN SOUP WITH GARLIC AND PARSLEY

INGREDIENTS

8 tbs extra-virgin olive oil
1 tsp chopped garlic
1.2 kg/2½ lbs tinned cannellini beans, drained and rinsed
salt
freshly ground black pepper
125 ml/4 fl oz tinned concentrated beef consommé, diluted in water to make 250 ml/ 8 fl oz stock
2 tbs finely chopped fresh parsley
thick slices of grilled crusty bread

This recipe comes from Marcella Hazan's beautiful book, The Essentials of Classic Italian Cooking. *It is a solid, nourishing soup with the authentic flavour of Italy, but it uses ingredients to be found in any well-stocked store cupboard. This is a soup with little liquid, almost solid enough to serve as a side dish. If you'd like it thinner, just add a little more stock or water.*

Put the oil and chopped garlic in a soup pot and turn the heat to medium. Sauté until the garlic becomes coloured a very pale gold. Add the beans, a pinch of salt, and a few grindings of pepper. Cover and simmer gently for 5 or 6 minutes.

Take a teacupful of beans from the pot, and purée them through a mouli or food processor. Return to the pot, add the stock, and simmer for another 5 or 6 minutes. Taste, correct for salt and pepper, swirl in the parsley, and turn off the heat. Ladle into individual soup bowls over the grilled bread slices.

Preparation time

5 minutes

Cooking time

20 minutes

Serves 4

CARROT SOUP

Preparation time

10 minutes

Cooking time

15 minutes

Serves 4

A fine pumpkin soup can be made the same way, but you will need much less liquid, and chicken or vegetable stock should be used instead of water to enhance the flavour.

Put the carrots and onion in a pan with the olive oil and the cloves. Stir, cover the pan, and let them heat through together over a low heat for 5 minutes. Then add the water and salt, and cook until the carrots are soft – about 10 minutes. Remove the cloves, blend or process, stir in the lemon juice, and add a swirl of cream or *fromage frais* and a sprinkle of parsley to each plate when you serve the dish.

INGREDIENTS
1 kg/2 lb carrots, finely chopped
1 large onion or 2 small ones, finely chopped
2 tbs extra-virgin olive oil
5 or 6 cloves
900 ml/1½ pt water
a little salt
juice of 1 lemon
To serve:
4 tbs single cream or *fromage frais*
1 tbs finely chopped fresh parsley

STILTON SOUP

Preparation time

5 minutes

Cooking time

20 minutes

Serves 4

Make this rich, delicious soup as a starter for a special meal, or as a meal on its own, with a crusty roll and a sharp green salad.

Heat the oil in a big pan, add the onion and celery, and sauté until they are just beginning to soften. Add the potato, water, and wine, and cook until the vegetables are done – about 15 minutes. Crumble in the Stilton, and heat through until it has melted into the soup. Then stir in the cream, reheat, and serve sprinkled with the parsley. Don't add salt – the Stilton will make the dish salty enough.

INGREDIENTS
1 tbs olive oil
1 large onion, finely chopped
2 stalks of celery, finely chopped
1 large potato or 3 or 4 small ones, peeled and diced
900 ml/1½ pt water
a glass of white wine
250 g/8 oz Stilton
150 ml/¼ pt single cream
To serve:
1 tbs finely chopped fresh parsley

COLD CUCUMBER AND YOGURT SOUP

INGREDIENTS

1 medium cucumber
salt
300 ml/½ pt plain yogurt
1 clove garlic, finely chopped
1 tsp white wine vinegar
a little fresh dill, chopped
salt and pepper
2 tsp olive oil
1 tsp lemon juice

Peel the cucumber, slice it paper-thin, and put to drain in a colander with a little salt sprinkled over it. After 10 minutes rinse it, and put it in a blender or food processor with the yogurt, garlic, vinegar, and dill. Blend thoroughly. Season to taste with salt and pepper, and chill. Serve with the oil and lemon juice dribbled over the surface.

Preparation time

5 minutes

Cooking time

30 minutes

Serves 4

ONION SOUP

INGREDIENTS

2 large Spanish onions
50 g/2 oz butter
1 tbs plain flour
900 ml/1½ pts chicken or vegetable stock
salt and freshly ground pepper
a little fresh thyme
4 thick slices wholemeal bread
125 g/4 oz grated cheese, use Gruyère or Cheddar

Peel the onions, and slice into rings. Heat the butter in a thick saucepan, add the onions, and sauté until they are just turning golden. Add the flour, and stir well. Heat the grill. Meanwhile, add the stock, salt, pepper, and thyme, and simmer gently for 10 minutes. Put the soup in an ovenproof casserole, and float the slices of bread on top. Sprinkle the cheese over them, and put under the grill until the cheese has melted.

Preparation time

10 minutes

Cooking time

25 minutes

Serves 4

EGG DISHES

PRESIA'S EGGS BOLOGNESE

Preparation time

5 minutes

Cooking time

15 minutes

Serves 4

Presia, the French wife of an Australian dental surgeon, is a marvellous cook with an individual, economical style. Her cooking is based on the very best ingredients – fresh vegetables and fruit, a little meat and fish, and good quality olive oil. This dish is a happy combination of the quick-to-prepare sauce used as the basis for Meatball and Tomato Sauce on page 122, eggs, and a potato or two to give it body. Omit the chilli if you don't like your food too hot. Make this dish in a wok.

Put the tomatoes and their juice in the wok with the crumbled stock cube, wine, onion, olive oil, chilli, and potatoes. Bring to simmering point, cover, and let it bubble away for 5–10 minutes, until the potatoes are soft. Add the herbs, stir, and break in the eggs carefully, so that the yolks don't break. Add a little salt and pepper on top of each egg, cover, and cook for another 5 minutes. Serve with plenty of wholewheat bread to mop up the sauce.

INGREDIENTS

400 g/14 oz can of chopped tomatoes
1 chicken or vegetable stock cube
2 tbs white wine
1 large onion, very finely chopped
2 tbs olive oil
1 fresh red or green chilli, deseeded and chopped
1 large or 2 medium potatoes, peeled and very finely chopped
1 tbs fresh parsley, basil, or coriander, chopped
4 eggs
salt and freshly ground black pepper

EGGS IN ONION SAUCE

Preparation time

5 minutes

Cooking time

25 minutes

Serves 4

Melt the butter in a pan, add the onion, and sauté until soft – about 10 minutes. Add the flour, and stir to a smooth paste. Add the milk a little at a time, stirring continuously, and cook for another 5–10 minutes. Put the halved eggs in an ovenproof dish, cover with the sauce, add the parsley, sprinkle with the wheatgerm, and put under a hot grill for 2 or 3 minutes until bubbling and golden.

INGREDIENTS

4 hard-boiled eggs, halved
25 g/1 oz butter
1 large onion, finely sliced
1 tbs wholewheat flour
450 ml/¾ pt milk
fresh parsley, chopped
1 tbs wheatgerm

SPANISH OMELETTE

INGREDIENTS

4 tbs olive oil

2 large potatoes, peeled and diced small

2 medium onions, finely sliced

3 eggs, well beaten

salt and freshly ground black pepper

One of the most popular items on Spanish beach-café menus, this omelette should be thick and quite solid, but still a little soft when you cut into it. It is also very good served cold, and makes excellent buffet food.

Heat the oil in a non-stick frying pan, put in the potatoes, and fry for a few minutes. Then add the onions, stir to coat them in the oil, cover the pan, turn the heat down, and cook gently for about 10 minutes, or until the potatoes and onions are soft. The onions should not brown. Remove the potatoes and onions from the pan, add to the beaten eggs, and season with a little salt and pepper. Drain off excess oil from the pan, tip in the egg mixture, and cook over a low heat for about 10 minutes, until it has set underneath. Using a big plate, turn the omelette over, and fry it for a minute on the other side.

Preparation time

5 minutes

Cooking time

25 minutes

Serves 4

COURGETTE OMELETTE GRATIN

INGREDIENTS

1 tbs olive oil

500 g/1 lb young, tender courgettes, cleaned and finely sliced

4 eggs

sea salt and freshly ground black pepper

2 tbs grated cheese – Cheddar, Parmesan, or another hard cheese

a sprinkling of *fines herbes*

Heat the grill. Heat the oil in a non-stick pan. Gently fry the courgettes until they are just beginning to take colour. Lightly beat the eggs, season with salt and pepper, and pour over the courgettes in the pan. Cook for a minute or two until the underside is set. Sprinkle with the cheese and the *fines herbes*, and grill until the top bubbles and becomes golden brown.

Preparation time

5 minutes

Cooking time

10 minutes

Serves 4

ODDS AND ENDS EGGS

Preparation time

10 minutes

Cooking time

10 minutes

Serves 2

Here is a delicious way to use up the odds and ends that are usually left over in your refrigerator, just before the big weekly shop.

Heat the oven to 200°C/400°F/gas 6, and heat the grill. Heat the oil in a pan, sauté the bacon, pepper, onion, and spring onions together until the vegetables have softened. Add the mushrooms, and sauté for another minute or two. Divide half the mixture between two ramekins, crack an egg into each, and spoon in – gently, so as not to break the yolks – the rest of the mixture. Sprinkle both with the grated cheese. Put in the hot oven for 3 minutes, then under the grill for another minute.

INGREDIENTS
2 tbs olive oil
2 or 3 rashers of streaky bacon, cut into small pieces
1 red pepper, ribbed, deseeded, and chopped
1 medium onion, finely chopped
a few spring onions, chopped
3 or 4 mushrooms, cleaned and chopped
2 eggs
50 g/2 oz Cheddar cheese, grated

BREAD AND CHEESE BAKE

Preparation time

10 minutes

Cooking time

30 minutes

Serves 4

Heat the oven to 200°C/400°F/gas 6. Butter the bread, and cut into smallish squares. Butter a pie dish. Put a layer of bread in the dish, top with the onion, then the cheese, and then make one more layer of bread, onion, and cheese. Whisk the eggs with the milk, season with salt and pepper, and pour over the dish. Bake for about 30 minutes until nicely brown on top.

INGREDIENTS
50 g/2 oz butter
4 slices wholemeal bread, crusts removed
1 onion, finely chopped
175 g/6 oz grated hard cheese
4 eggs
600 ml/1 pt milk
salt and pepper

BREAD AND CHEESE WITH EGGS

INGREDIENTS

1 tbs butter

4–6 slices wholewheat bread, crusts removed

3 tomatoes, sliced

175 g/6 oz cheese – Cheddar, Gruyère, or Emmenthal, thinly sliced

6 eggs

salt and freshly ground black pepper

Heat the oven to 200°C/400°F/gas 6. Generously butter a shallow ovenproof dish. Line it with the bread. Cover the bread with a layer of sliced tomatoes and then a layer of cheese. Break the eggs on top. Add a little salt and pepper. Bake for 15 minutes, or until the egg whites are set.

Preparation time

5 minutes

Cooking time

15 minutes

Serves 4

EGGS MORNAY

INGREDIENTS

1 tbs butter

4 eggs

Sauce Mornay (p.145)

1 tbs grated Cheddar or other sharp cheese

Heat the oven to 190°C/375°F/gas 5. Butter a fireproof casserole, break the 4 eggs carefully into it, and top with the Sauce Mornay. Sprinkle the cheese on top, and put in the oven for 5 minutes.

Preparation time

7 minutes

Cooking time

5 minutes

Serves 4

SCRAMBLED EGGS WITH SMOKED HADDOCK

Preparation time

5 minutes

Cooking time

12 minutes

Serves 2

Cook the haddock in the milk for 2 or 3 minutes, then strain, and save the milk. Flake the haddock, discarding skin and bones, and keep it hot. Beat the eggs with 2 tablespoonfuls of the fishy milk, and season with a little pepper, but don't add salt. Melt the butter in a non-stick pan. Add the eggs, and stir briskly off the heat. Just before the eggs set add the flaked haddock, and stir it in.

INGREDIENTS

175 g/6 oz smoked haddock – avoid the lurid yellow kind
150 ml/¼ pt milk
4 eggs
freshly ground black pepper
1 tbs butter
To serve:
hot wholewheat toast

EGGS TONNATO

Preparation time

5 minutes

Cooking time

10 minutes

Serves 4

This can be either a substantial starter, or a light meal in itself. In the latter case you may wish to use a few more eggs.

Hard-boil the eggs for 10 minutes. Shell the eggs, halve them, and arrange them face-down in a flat salad bowl. Drain the tuna, flake it, and add to the mayonnaise. Stir in the onion and 1 tablespoon of the parsley – save a little to garnish. Season to taste with salt and pepper. Spoon the mayonnaise over the eggs, and sprinkle with the rest of the parsley.

INGREDIENTS

4 eggs
200 g/7 oz can tuna
6 tbs mayonnaise
1 small onion, finely chopped
2 tbs fresh parsley, chopped
salt and pepper

BAKED EGGS AND MUSHROOMS

INGREDIENTS

1 tbs butter
250 g/8 oz mushrooms, thinly sliced
1½ tbs flour
450 ml/¾ pt chicken or vegetable stock
1½ tbs single cream
salt and freshly ground black pepper
1 tbs fresh parsley, chopped
4 eggs
1 tbs grated Cheddar cheese

Heat the oven to 200°C/400°F/gas 6. Melt the butter in a non-stick pan. Add the sliced mushrooms, and toss for 1 or 2 minutes. Stir in the flour. Toss again, and add the stock. Cook gently for 5 minutes, add the cream, salt and pepper, and parsley. Transfer to an ovenproof dish. Break in the eggs, and sprinkle with the grated cheese. Place in the oven for about 5 minutes, or until the whites of the eggs are set.

Preparation time

2 minutes

Cooking time

20 minutes

Serves 4

RED AND YELLOW EGGS

INGREDIENTS

1 large red pepper
1 large yellow pepper
1 medium onion
3 or 4 ripe red tomatoes
50 g/2 oz butter
6 eggs
salt and freshly ground black pepper
1 tbs fresh parsley, chopped

Halve the peppers, remove the ribs and seeds, and slice into fat strips. Finely chop the onion. Skin and roughly chop the tomatoes. Heat the butter in a non-stick pan. Add the peppers and onion, and stew gently, covered, until they are softened, or for about 10 minutes. Stir in the tomatoes, and cook for about another 5 minutes. Beat the eggs, season with salt and pepper, and add the parsley. Add to the vegetable mixture, and stir until the eggs are just set.

Preparation time

5 minutes

Cooking time

15 minutes

Serves 4

FISH

PRAWN, BROCCOLI, AND LEEK STIR-FRY

Preparation time

10 minutes

Cooking time

15 minutes

Serves 2

Any green vegetable, such as beans, mange-tout, or spinach, can be added to this recipe.

Heat the oil in a large frying pan or wok, and quickly fry, but do not brown, the garlic. Add the broccoli, and cook for 2 minutes, then add the leeks, and cook for another minute, stirring constantly. Stir in the soy sauce, stock, and tomato. Mix the flour with 2 tablespoonfuls of water to make a smooth paste, and stir into the sauce. Cook until thickened. Add the prawns, carrot, and ginger, and cook over a rapid heat for 1 minute. Stir in the watercress, and serve immediately.

INGREDIENTS
2 tbs sunflower oil
1 clove garlic, crushed
125 g/4 oz small broccoli florets
1 leek, finely sliced
1 tbs dark soy sauce
4 tbs vegetable stock
1 tomato, chopped
1 tbs plain flour
125 g/4 oz cooked prawns
1 carrot, peeled and cut into thin matchsticks
2.5 cm/1 in root ginger, cut into thin matchsticks
75 g/3 oz fresh watercress

SCALLOPS AND PRAWNS PROVENÇALE

Preparation time

10 minutes

Cooking time

10 minutes

Serves 4

Boiled brown rice, seasoned with a lump of butter and a tablespoonful of lemon juice, goes well with this dish. Serve with a green vegetable or salad.

Wash the scallops, remove the corals, and slice the flesh into 3 or 4 pieces. Slice the corals. Wash and blot dry the prawns. Sprinkle them with lemon juice and seasoning, and dust them very lightly with flour. Heat the oil and butter, add the scallops, and allow them to take colour. Add the prawns, and fry until the scallops are just beginning to turn golden, and the prawns brown. Add the coral slices, toss for a minute or two longer, then stir in the garlic and parsley. Toss together and serve.

INGREDIENTS
6 scallops
250 g/8 oz fresh prawns
1 tbs lemon juice
sea salt and freshly ground black pepper
flour for dusting
2 tbs olive oil
1 tbs butter
2 cloves garlic, chopped
2 tbs fresh parsley, finely chopped

PRAWN AND TOMATO CURRY

INGREDIENTS

1 medium onion, chopped
400 g/14 oz tin of tomatoes
1 clove garlic, chopped
2 tbs fresh coriander, chopped
3 tbs frozen peas
½ chicken or vegetable stock cube
1 tsp ground cumin
1 tsp ground coriander
a good squeeze of tomato paste from a tube
salt
1 tsp garam masala
2 tbs curry powder
1 red chilli, deseeded and chopped
375 g/12 oz prawns, shelled and cooked (if using frozen, defrost in the fridge all day)
150 ml/¼ pt single cream

To make this a more substantial dish, add a tin of sweetcorn in unsweetened water to the tomato sauce.

Put the onion, tomatoes with their juice, garlic, half of the fresh coriander, frozen peas, and crumbled stock cube in a pan. Let them simmer for about 5 minutes.

Make a paste with the cumin, ground coriander, tomato paste, salt, and a little water. Add the garam masala, curry powder, and chilli. Add this mixture to the tomato sauce, and simmer for about 5 minutes.

Add the prawns, and let them simmer in the sauce for a further 3 minutes – no longer or they will go leathery. Then turn off the heat, stir in the cream, sprinkle with the rest of the fresh coriander, and serve at once with plain boiled rice.

Preparation time

5 minutes

Cooking time

15 minutes

Serves 4

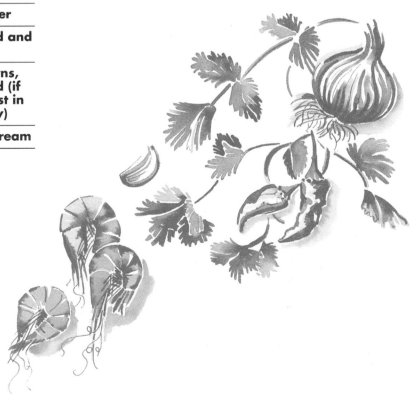

POTTED PRAWNS

Preparation time

10 minutes

Serves 4

A tasty, protein-rich snack, that will keep in your refrigerator for 2 or 3 days. You can also prepare shrimps this way.

Melt the butter in a small pan. Add the spices and lemon juice, and leave to stand off the heat for 10 minutes. Put the prawns in a small china pot, and strain the seasoned butter over them through a piece of muslin. Press down, and store in the fridge. Serve with the toast, lemon, and a sprinkle of paprika.

INGREDIENTS
125 g/4 oz butter
a good pinch of cayenne pepper
1 level tsp ground mace
1 level tsp grated nutmeg
1 tsp lemon juice
500 g/1 lb cooked prawns – you can use frozen
To serve:
wholewheat toast
lemon quarters
paprika

COD WITH A SESAME SEED COATING ON A BED OF WARM SPINACH

Preparation time

5 minutes

Cooking time

25 minutes

Serves 2

This is a highly nutritious variation on the egg-and-breadcrumbed fish theme.

Heat the oven to 175°C/350°F/gas 4. Place the sesame seeds on a large, flat plate. Season the fish with salt and pepper, and brush with beaten egg. Press the sesame seeds over the sides of the fish, brushing with extra egg if necessary. Place the fish well apart on a baking sheet, and cook in the oven for 20 minutes.

Just before serving, melt the butter in a large frying pan, and add the spinach leaves. Over a high heat stir the leaves until they are just wilting. Add the nutmeg, a little salt and pepper to taste, and the *crème fraîche*. Mix carefully. Divide between two plates, and rest the cod on top. Serve with wedges of lemon.

INGREDIENTS
50 g/2 oz sesame seeds
2 fish steaks – cod or other firm, white fish
salt and freshly ground black pepper
1 egg, beaten
For the spinach:
a knob of butter
250 g/8 oz young spinach leaves
freshly grated nutmeg
salt and freshly ground black pepper
2 tbs *crème fraîche*

PEPPER-CRUSTED FISH IN A WARM LIME AND CORIANDER VINAIGRETTE

INGREDIENTS

1 heaped tbs mixed peppercorns, coarsley crushed

1 heaped tbs plain flour, seasoned with a little salt

2 fresh or frozen white fish fillets, each weighing approx. 200 g/7 oz

1 tbs olive oil

For the vinaigrette:

1 clove garlic, peeled

2 level tsp coarse-grain mustard

grated rind and juice of 2 limes

4 tbs olive oil

salt and freshly ground black pepper

fresh coriander leaves, chopped

This delicious recipe was presented in a leaflet by a British supermarket to their customers.

Mix together the peppercorns and seasoned flour. Skin the fish fillets, wipe with kitchen paper, and coat them with the peppercorn mixture, pressing it well onto both sides. Set aside.

Meanwhile, prepare the vinaigrette. Crush the garlic in a bowl, and stir in the mustard, lime rind and juice, 4 tablespoons olive oil, seasoning, and coriander.

Heat a tablespoonful of olive oil in a large frying pan. When hot, add the fish and fry for 3 minutes on each side, until crisp and golden. Keeping the heat high, pour the vinaigrette around the fish, and maintain heat for a couple of minutes to reduce the liquid.

Preparation time

10 minutes

Cooking time

8 minutes

Serves 2

GRILLED FISH WITH CHEESE

INGREDIENTS

1 fish steak per person, cod or another firm, white fish

salt and pepper

a knob of butter

Dijon mustard

1 tbs grated Cheddar cheese

Pat the fish steaks dry, and season them with salt and pepper. Line the grill pan with foil, and heat the grill to maximum. Melt the butter in the grill pan, put the fish steaks in, and turn them immediately. Paint the upper sides with mustard, sprinkle the grated cheese on top, and grill for a few minutes, until the steaks are cooked through.

Preparation time

5 minutes

Cooking time

10 minutes

Serves 1

SALMON EN PAPILLOTE

Preparation time

10 minutes

Cooking time

15–20 minutes

Serves 4

This is an impressive, but incredibly simple, recipe to prepare – an ideal choice for dinner parties. You could use foil instead of paper, but then you wouldn't want to present the fish wrapped at the table, which is part of the impact.

Heat the oven to 200°C/400°F/gas 6. Cut 4 pieces of greaseproof paper large enough to wrap around the fish. Brush lightly with oil and place the fish in the centre. Scatter the herbs, capers, and anchovies over the fish, season with salt and pepper, a squeeze of lemon juice and a drizzle of olive oil. Fold the paper around the fish to form a secure parcel – you can staple it together – place on a baking tray, and cook it for 15–20 minutes, depending on the thickness of the fish.

INGREDIENTS
4 salmon steaks or fillets
1 or 2 tbs olive oil
3 tbs chopped fresh tarragon
2 tbs chopped fresh flat-leaf parsley
1 tbs capers, chopped
small tin anchovies, drained and chopped
salt and freshly ground black pepper
lemon juice, to taste

FISH BAKED IN A PARCEL

Preparation time

10 minutes

Cooking time

20 minutes

Serves 4

Heat the oven to 200°C/400°F/gas 6. Stuff the fish with most of the dill and fennel, half the lemon, and half the butter. Add a little salt, and grind in a little pepper. Put the fish on a large sheet of baking parchment, and arrange the rest of the dill, fennel, and lemon slices on top. Cut the remaining butter into pieces, and dot the fish with it. Sprinkle over a little salt and pepper.

Fold over the baking parchment and make it into a parcel, tying up both ends with string. Bake for about 20 minutes – it is done when the paper starts to turn brown. Serve with new potatoes and a green salad.

INGREDIENTS
1 sea bass or salmon trout, weighing approx. 1 kg/2 lb, cleaned
a handful of fresh dill
a handful of fresh fennel fronds
1 lemon, sliced
50 g/2 oz butter
salt and pepper

SALT-BAKED FISH

INGREDIENTS

1 whole fish, cleaned and gutted

approx. 1 kg/2 lbs rock salt

This is a fast, easy – and mercifully odourless – way to cook a beautiful whole fish, such as sea bass, bream, or grey mullet. It will emerge firm, fresh-tasting, and fragrant. Needless to say, only the finest and freshest of fish should be cooked this way.

Heat the oven to 200°C/400°F/gas 6. Spread half of the salt in a roasting tin, and lay the fish on it. Cover the fish with the rest of the salt. When the oven is fully heated, bake the fish for about 20 minutes. The salt will solidify and start to crack. Break it open carefully, and transfer the fish to a serving dish. Serve with Quick Garlic Mayonnaise *(see page 146)* or Tomato and Lemon Salsa *(see page 144).*

Preparation time

2 minutes

Cooking time

20 minutes

Serves 4

FAR EASTERN FISH

INGREDIENTS

750 g/1½ lb fresh, firm fish steaks or fillets – use cod, haddock, halibut, or coley

salt

5 tbs groundnut oil

1 small onion, finely chopped

4–6 spring onions, cleaned and finely chopped – include plenty of the green stalks

1 tbs fresh ginger root, grated

2 tbs each light and dark soy sauce

2 tsp white sugar

125 ml/4 fl oz chicken or vegetable stock

This classic Chinese recipe for fish simmered in an aromatic soy-based sauce is best done in a non-stick frying pan.

Wash and blot dry the fish, then cut into big pieces. Heat the oil in a pan. Add the fish, and brown it. Remove it, and put it to drain on kitchen paper. Pour off most of the remaining oil, add the onions and the spring onions, and fry for a minute. Add the ginger, soy sauces, sugar, salt, and stock, and heat to boiling point. Turn the heat down, put the fish back in the pan, cover, and simmer for about 5 minutes. Take out the fish, put it in a serving dish, and pour the sauce over. Serve with plain boiled rice.

Preparation time

8 minutes

Cooking time

10 minutes

Serves 4

GRILLED RED MULLET

Preparation time

5 minutes

Cooking time

10 minutes

Serves 2

Quarter the radicchio, and cut out the thick stem. Heat the grill, and grill the mullet for just 3 minutes on each side. Mix together the oil, garlic, and herbs, and place the grilled mullet in the mixture to cool. Brush the radicchio with a little of the marinade oil, and grill until it begins to wilt and turn brown. Serve the mullet on top of the radicchio.

INGREDIENTS
1 head of red radicchio
2 red mullet, cleaned
100 ml/3 fl oz olive oil
2 cloves garlic, chopped
1 tsp chopped fresh thyme or oregano, or a pinch of dried *herbes de Provence*

FISH WITH MUSHROOMS

Preparation time

10 minutes

Cooking time

30 minutes

Serves 4

Heat the oven to 190°C/375°F/gas 5. Butter a shallow casserole, and put in the fish. Melt 1 tablespoonful of butter in a frying pan over a very low heat, and gently fry the shallots and mushrooms. Season with a little salt and pepper, and cook together for a few minutes. Then cover the fish with the onion and mushroom mixture, and pour over the wine. Cook in the oven for 20–25 minutes. Just before serving, sprinkle over the lemon juice and the parsley.

INGREDIENTS
1½ tbs butter
4 fish steaks
2 or 3 shallots or small onions, finely chopped
10–12 mushrooms, sliced
salt and pepper
1 glass dry white wine
1 tsp lemon juice
1 tbs fresh parsley, chopped

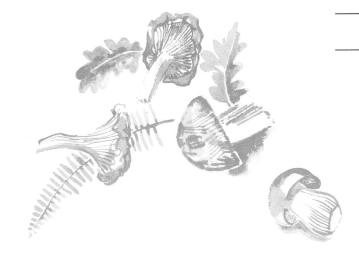

FISHCAKES

INGREDIENTS

200 g/7 oz tin of salmon, mackerel, or tuna

1 tbs butter or oil

1 small onion, finely chopped

2 slices wholewheat bread, crusts removed

1 egg, beaten

1 tsp fresh dill, chopped

2 tbs fresh parsley, chopped

flour for dusting

1 lemon, quartered

Drain the fish, and remove any skin or bits of bone. Heat the butter or oil in a pan, and sauté the onion until it is soft. Put the fish in a mixing bowl. Process the bread to crumbs, and add them, with the onion, beaten egg, and herbs to the mixing bowl. Mix together thoroughly. Form the mixture into 4 flat cakes, dust with flour, and sauté in the remaining butter and oil until golden-brown on both sides. Serve with quarters of lemon.

Preparation time

10 minutes

Cooking time

15 minutes

Serves 4

FRIED FISH WITH A TOMATO SAUCE

INGREDIENTS

4 fillets of fish – hake or another firm, white fish

1 egg

1 tbs flour

salt and freshly ground black pepper

2 tbs oil

Spicy Tomato and Onion Sauce (p.145)

Clean the fish, and blot it dry. Beat the egg, and spread the flour, seasoned with salt and pepper, on a plate. Heat the oil in a frying pan. Dip the slices of hake in the egg, then in the flour and fry for 2 or 3 minutes on each side. Serve with the tomato sauce. Alternatively, you can serve the fish with quarters of lemon and a green salad.

Preparation time

5 minutes

Cooking time

4–6 minutes

Serves 4

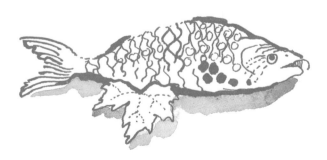

DEVILLED SARDINES

Preparation time

5 minutes

Cooking time

5 minutes

Serves 1

Heat the grill. Wash the sardines, and pat them dry with kitchen paper. Brush them with mustard, and sprinkle a little cayenne on both sides. Grill for about 2 minutes each side. Serve immediately with the lemon wedges and toast.

INGREDIENTS

2 or 3 fresh sardines per person, gutted

Dijon mustard

cayenne pepper

To serve:

lemon wedges

hot toast

GRILLED SARDINES WITH MUSTARD AND YOGURT SAUCE

Preparation time

5 minutes

Cooking time

5 minutes

Serves 4

Heat the grill to maximum, and line the grill pan with foil. Brush the sardines with the oil, and grill them for a couple of minutes on each side. Stir the mustard and parsley into the yogurt or *fromage frais*. Serve the grilled sardines with this sauce on the side, and the lemon quarters.

INGREDIENTS

3 or 4 sardines per person, cleaned

a little olive oil

1 tbs Dijon mustard

1 tbs fresh parsley, finely chopped

150 g/5 oz plain yogurt or *fromage frais*

To serve:

lemon quarters

MARINATED FISH I

INGREDIENTS

2 or 3 ripe tomatoes, chopped fairly small

a handful of fresh dill, parsley, or fennel fronds, finely chopped

1 small onion, finely chopped

salt and freshly ground black pepper

3 tbs olive oil

4 fish fillets – you can use frozen fish

Heat the oven to 200°C/400°F/gas 6. Put the chopped tomatoes in a wide, shallow dish with the herbs, onion, seasoning, and oil. Put the fillets in this marinade, and leave for 15 minutes. Then take them out, and put aside.

Cut 4 sheets of foil big enough to enclose each fillet. Put a small spoonful of the mixture in the middle of each piece of foil. Lay the fillets on top, and divide the rest of the mixture between them. Seal up by folding the foil and twisting the edges together. Bake in the hot oven for 15 minutes.

Preparation time

5 minutes

Marinating time

15 minutes

Cooking time

15 minutes

Serves 4

MARINATED FISH II

INGREDIENTS

4 tbs olive oil

1 small onion, finely chopped

juice of a lime (or lemon, if you can't find a lime)

a handful of finely chopped fresh dill, parsley, or fennel fronds

salt and freshly ground black pepper

4 fish steaks or fillets – you can use frozen fish

2 tbs grated Parmesan cheese, or 4 tbs grated Cheddar cheese

Make the marinade by mixing the olive oil, onion, lime juice, herbs, and seasoning in a wide, shallow dish. Add the fish, and let it marinate for 15 minutes – or longer, if you prefer.

Five minutes before you're ready to cook, heat the grill. Spread a sheet of foil in the grill pan, oil it very lightly, then put in the fish fillets, and spoon a little of the marinade over them. Grill for 5 minutes, turn over, and grill for 5 minutes on the other side. Sprinkle over the grated cheese, and grill for another 2 or 3 minutes, until the cheese bubbles.

Preparation time

5 minutes

Marinating time

15 minutes

Cooking time

13 minutes

Serves 4

MEAT AND POULTRY

ITALIAN-STYLE STEAK IN RED WINE

Preparation time

2 minutes

Cooking time

10 minutes

Serves 4

Heat a large frying pan, and add the oil and butter. Put the flour onto a shallow plate, and coat the steaks. When the butter stops foaming, add the garlic and the steaks. Cook over a medium heat for 1 minute each side, remove with a slotted spoon, and set aside. Add the wine, turn up the heat, and cook until most of it has evaporated, stirring constantly with a wooden spoon to loosen the pieces from the bottom of the pan. Season the steaks with salt and pepper, return to the pan, and cook for a further 2 or 3 minutes each side, depending on how rare you like your meat.

Enjoy the steaks with the rest of the wine.

INGREDIENTS

2 tbs oil
25 g/1 oz butter
4 tbs plain flour
4 fillet steaks, approx. 2.5 cm/1 in thick
2 cloves garlic, crushed and peeled
250 ml/8 fl oz full-bodied red wine – Chianti, Barolo, or Barbera
a little salt and freshly ground black pepper

HENRI'S MEDITERRANEAN STEAK

Preparation time

10 minutes

Cooking time

10 minutes

Serves 2

Heat the grill, and line the grill pan with a piece of foil, turned up at the edge so that the cooking juices can't run away. Brush the steaks on both sides with the garlic and Dijon mustard, and set aside.

Pour 1 tablespoonful of the oil into the lined grill pan, heat under the grill for a minute, add the peppers and onions, stir them around in the oil, and add the remaining oil. Sprinkle with a pinch of *fines herbes*, or oregano. Grill for 4 or 5 minutes, or until the onions are just beginning to look translucent, and the pepper is beginning to soften.

Put the steaks on top, return to the grill, and grill for 3 or 4 minutes. Turn the steaks over, and grill for another 3 or 4 minutes, depending on how well cooked you like your steaks. Serve with the pepper and onion mixture, and the delicious pan juices.

INGREDIENTS

2 rump or sirloin steaks
1 clove garlic, crushed
2 tsp Dijon mustard
2 tbs olive oil
1 medium red pepper, deseeded, deribbed, and finely sliced
1 medium onion, sliced
a pinch of dried *fines herbes*, or oregano

BEEF STIR-FRY

INGREDIENTS

375 g/12 oz rump, sirloin, or fillet steak, cut into very thin strips
1 level tbs cornflour
¼ tsp Chinese five spice
3 tbs light or dark soy sauce
175 g/6 oz broccoli
2 tbs sesame oil
1 tbs chopped fresh ginger
1 clove garlic, finely chopped
1 red pepper, thinly sliced
1 bunch salad onions, sliced diagonally
4 or 5 tbs sherry

Place the steak in a bowl with the cornflour, Chinese five spice, and soy sauce. Mix well, and leave to marinate for 20 minutes.

Split the broccoli into florets, slice the stalks diagonally into thin oval shapes, and the florets into small heads. Heat the oil in a wok or large frying pan, add the marinated steak, the ginger and garlic, and stir-fry for 3 or 4 minutes. Add the pepper, broccoli, and salad onions, and stir-fry for 2 minutes. Add the sherry and 2 tablespoonfuls of water, put a lid on the pan, and steam for 1 minute. Put in a warmed serving dish, and serve immediately with rice or egg noodles.

Preparation time

15 minutes

Cooking time

10 minutes

Serves 4

ITALIAN PAN-FRIED LIVER

INGREDIENTS

5 tbs sunflower oil
25 g/1 oz butter
1 onion, coarsely chopped
2 rashers bacon, stretched with the back of a knife, and cut in 2
salt and pepper
375 g/12 oz calf's liver, thinly sliced
2 or 3 tbs fino, or dry sherry
a handful of chopped parsley

The last-minute addition of dry sherry makes a delicious sauce, but if no sherry is to be found, use vermouth, or failing that, just water.

Heat the oil and butter together until foaming, and add the onion. Cook until softened and beginning to brown. Remove the onion, and add the bacon. Cook until just beginning to brown, then remove. Season the liver with salt and pepper, and sauté it over a high heat for 1 minute on either side, or until it is just turning brown. Return the onions and bacon to the pan, and pour in the sherry. Heat until bubbling, and a sauce has formed. Stir in the parsley, and serve immediately, while the liver is still pink.

Preparation time

5 minutes

Cooking time

20 minutes

Serves 2

LAMB AND PINE KERNEL KOFTAS

Preparation time

5 minutes

Cooking time

5 minutes

Serves 4

Heat the grill to maximum. Place the onion and pine kernels in a food processor, and chop finely. Add the lamb, mint, and egg, and blend to a smooth paste. Shape into walnut-sized balls, or into small sausage shapes, and press tightly onto kebab sticks. Grill for 2 minutes on each side. Serve with the pitta bread, lemon wedges, and green salad.

INGREDIENTS

1 onion, chopped

50 g/2 oz pine kernels

500 g/1 lb minced lamb

1 tbs chopped fresh mint

1 egg, beaten

To serve:

wholewheat pita bread

lemon wedges

**green salad leaves –
rocket, watercress,
and cos**

LAMB BURGERS

Preparation time

5 minutes

Cooking time

10 minutes

Serves 4

Soak the bread in water, then squeeze out the excess water. If you have a food processor you can simply put in all the other ingredients and process them briefly – chop the onion finely first. But it's quite easy to mix them by hand. Crumble the bread into a bowl with the minced lamb. Some supermarkets sell low-fat, ready-minced lamb, or you can buy fillets, and mince them in a food processor. Add the finely chopped onion. Beat the egg, and add it. Add the herbs, seasonings, and mix. At this point the mixture can be left to gather flavour for 2 or 3 hours if you like, or you can leave it all day in the refrigerator in a bowl covered with cling film.

When you're ready to cook, heat the grill to maximum, shape the lamb mixture into burgers, oil the grill rack, and grill for 3 or 4 minutes on each side. Serve with a tomato sauce *(see pages 144–145)*.

INGREDIENTS

**a slice of wholemeal
bread with the crusts
removed**

500 g/1 lb minced lamb

1 large onion

1 egg

**a good pinch of dried
oregano**

**a good pinch of dried
thyme**

**1 tbs chopped fresh
parsley**

1 tbs chopped fresh mint

**salt and freshly ground
black pepper**

LAMB PEPERONATA

INGREDIENTS

| 3 tbs olive oil |
| 1 large onion, coarsely chopped |
| 4 lamb chops |
| 3 or 4 big, ripe tomatoes |
| 1 red pepper and 1 yellow pepper, deseeded, deribbed, and sliced |
| a good pinch vegetable stock powder |
| salt and pepper |

Heat the oil, add the onion, and fry until soft. Remove the onion with a slotted spoon, and fry the lamb chops until nicely browned on both sides. Remove the chops, and return the onions to the pan. Add the tomatoes, skinned and chopped, peppers, 2 tablespoonfuls of water if necessary, and the stock powder. Season to taste, and cook for about 15 minutes. Return the chops to the pan, cover, and cook for another 5 minutes.

Preparation time

5 minutes

Cooking time

30 minutes

Serves 4

GRILLED PAPRIKA CHICKEN

INGREDIENTS

| 1 tsp paprika |
| a good sprinkling of freshly ground black pepper |
| juice and grated rind of 1 large unwaxed lemon |
| 2 tbs olive oil |
| 1 clove garlic, finely chopped |
| 4 medium-sized chicken breasts, skinned, and cut into bite-sized cubes |
| *To serve:* |
| **Grilled Tomatoes (p.135)** |
| **crusty brown rolls** |

Heat the grill. Mix together the paprika, pepper, lemon, oil, and garlic. Put the chicken pieces into this mixture, and leave to marinate in the fridge for 10 minutes or longer.

Line the grill pan with foil, and brush the rack with oil. Remove the chicken pieces from the marinade with a slotted spoon, and grill them for 10–12 minutes, turning them from time to time, and basting them with the marinade.

Serve with Grilled Tomatoes and bread rolls to mop up the delicious pan juices.

Preparation time

15 minutes

Cooking time

15 minutes

Serves 4

SPICY CHICKEN WINGS

Preparation time

5 minutes

Marinating time

15 minutes

Cooking time

12 minutes

Serves 4

Put the chicken wings in a flat dish. Mix together all the other ingredients and pour over the chicken. Leave to marinate for 15 minutes, turning the chicken wings a few times in the sauce.

Heat the grill, and line the grill pan with foil. Cook the chicken wings for 10–12 minutes, turning them 2 or 3 times, and basting them with the remaining marinade. Serve with a large mixed salad – and plenty of paper napkins, as the only way to eat these is with your fingers – and a glass of cold beer. This is also a great dish for the barbecue.

INGREDIENTS

750 g/1½ lb chicken wings, with the tips removed

8 tbs tomato ketchup

3 tbs Worcestershire sauce

1 tbs runny honey

3 tsp paprika

3 tsp English dried mustard powder

1 tsp turmeric

salt and freshly ground black pepper

CHICKEN WITH GARLIC

Preparation time

2 minutes

Cooking time

25–30 minutes

Serves 4

Good for the heart, not for the faint-hearted.

Heat the oil and butter in a large, deep frying pan. Season the chicken, add it to the pan, and cook until it is evenly brown on both sides for 8–10 minutes. Reduce the heat, and place the unpeeled cloves of garlic under the chicken on the bottom of the pan. Cook for a further 10 minutes, shaking the pan regularly, then add the wine, and scrape all the cooking bits from around the pan with a wooden spoon. Continue cooking for another 8–10 minutes until the chicken is thoroughly done.

Arrange the golden garlic around the pieces of chicken, and sprinkle with the parsley. Serve with the bread and the rest of the dry white wine.

INGREDIENTS

3 tbs extra-virgin olive oil

15 g/½ oz butter

4 leg quarters of chicken

salt and plenty of freshly ground black pepper

at least 10 large cloves garlic – up to 30 if you're brave!

300 ml/½ pt dry white wine

1 tbs chopped fresh parsley

To serve:

thick chunks of bread

CHICKEN NASI GORENG

INGREDIENTS

375 g/12 oz easy-cook rice
2 tbs sesame oil
500 g/1 lb chicken breasts, skinned and diced
1 large carrot, sliced very thinly
1 medium green pepper, deseeded, and sliced very thinly
2 tsp Chinese five spice
½ tsp ground coriander
a pinch of cayenne pepper
2.5 cm/1 in piece of fresh ginger, peeled and grated
2 cloves garlic, peeled and finely chopped
4 tbs soy sauce
250 g/8 oz fresh beansprouts
4 good-sized spring onions, sliced thinly lengthways

This is a delicious Indonesian recipe that makes a complete meal on its own.

While the rice is cooking, prepare the other ingredients. Heat the oil in a wok, and stir-fry the chicken for 4 minutes. Add the carrot and green pepper, and continue to cook for another 2 minutes. Add all the spices, and stir briskly. Add the rest of the ingredients and the cooked, drained rice. Cook for a further 3 minutes, stirring vigorously.

Preparation time

10 minutes

Cooking time

20 minutes

Serves 4

CHICKEN JALFREZI

This recipe, from the Lal Quila Restaurant in Surrey, England, is quoted in Favourite Restaurant Curries, *by Pat Chapman.*

Preparation time

10 minutes

Cooking time

20 minutes

Serves 4

Heat the oil in a large frying pan, or better still, a wok. Add the cumin seeds, stir, add the garlic, and stir for half a minute. Add the ginger, stir for another half a minute, add the turmeric, a tablespoon of water, and then the curry paste.

Add the chicken pieces, and stir continuously for another 2 minutes. Add the chillis, pepper, tomatoes, and cook for about 10 minutes, adding the coconut milk little by little. Add the garam masala and the coriander or parsley, and stir for 5 minutes. Make sure the chicken is cooked right through, and serve with the rice which can be cooked while you are preparing the rest of the meal.

INGREDIENTS

3 tbs sunflower seed oil
1 tsp cumin seeds
3 cloves garlic, peeled and chopped
2.5 cm/1 in piece fresh ginger, peeled and finely grated
1 tsp turmeric
4 tsp bottled mild curry paste
750 g/1½ lb chicken breast, skinned and cubed
2 fresh green chillis, deseeded and thinly sliced
1 medium red pepper, deseeded and cut into 2.5 cm/½ in cubes
10 cherry tomatoes, halved
100 ml/3 fl oz tinned coconut milk
1 level tbs garam masala
1 tbs chopped fresh parsley or coriander
375 g/12 oz easy-cook rice

DUCK BREASTS WITH ORANGE JUICE

INGREDIENTS

2 duck breasts with skin

juice of 2 oranges and rind of ½ orange

1 or 2 tbs clear honey

salt and freshly ground black pepper

Heat a large frying pan until hot. Prick the duck skin all over with a fork, and place skin-side down into the ungreased, but hot pan. Cover, and cook for 6 minutes. The fat will run out of the skin and can be poured away, and the skin will become crisp. Turn the duck breasts over, and cook for a further 2 minutes on the second side for pink flesh. (If you like your duck well done, or the duck breasts are large, you will need to cook them for longer.) Pour in the freshly squeezed orange juice, the orange rind, cut into very thin julienne strips, and the honey into the pan, and increase the heat. Season with salt and pepper, and as the liquid forms a thickish sauce, spoon it over the duck. Serve with crisp vegetables, such as mange-tout, or French beans.

Preparation time

5 minutes

Cooking time

10–15 minutes

Serves 2

DUCK BREASTS IN GREEN PEPPER SAUCE

INGREDIENTS

1 tbs butter

4 duck breasts

1 medium onion, very finely chopped

1 tbs green peppercorns

salt

½ glass dry sherry

100 ml/3 fl oz single cream

Heat the butter in a pan and fry the duck breasts for 3–5 minutes on each side until they are a rich brown colour. Remove the breasts, and keep them warm. Fry the onion in the butter over a moderate heat until it is just beginning to colour. Add the green peppercorns, a pinch of salt, and the sherry. Stir together, and simmer for 10 minutes. Add the cream, and simmer for another 2 or 3 minutes.

Meanwhile, cut the duck breasts into short strips, put them in a dish, and keep them warm. When the sauce is ready, pour it over the duck, and serve at once.

Preparation time

5 minutes

Cooking time

20 minutes

Serves 4

PRESIA'S TURKEY STIR-FRY

This tasty dish is just as good heated up the next day.

Preparation time

10 minutes

Cooking time

10 minutes

Serves 4

Heat the oil in a wok, and add the ginger, garlic, chilli, and the turkey. Stir-fry for 1½ minutes if the turkey is minced – longer if it is diced. Add the onion and the vegetables – you can use broccoli, baby corn, mange-tout, small carrots, sliced lengthways, Chinese cabbage, or cauliflower. Stir, and add the sesame oil for flavour. Stir-fry for another 3 or 4 minutes, sprinkling in the soy sauce until the ingredients are fuming and crackling. Turn off the heat.

Meanwhile, cook the egg noodles. Boil a panful of water, add the noodles, and immediately turn off the heat. Six minutes later they will be done. Add the black bean sauce and oyster sauce to the stir-fry, add the strained noodles, and serve.

INGREDIENTS

2 tbs peanut oil
2.5 cm/1 in piece of ginger root, finely sliced
10 cloves garlic, peeled
1 fresh chilli, deseeded and chopped finely
500 g/1 lb minced turkey, or diced lean turkey
1 small onion, cut finely
500 g/1 lb mixed vegetables, washed and chopped finely
½ tsp sesame oil
3 or 4 tbs soy sauce
egg noodles
1 tbs black bean sauce
1 tbs oyster sauce

CURRIED TURKEY

INGREDIENTS

3 tbs vegetable oil

2 medium onions, finely chopped

4 fat garlic cloves, finely chopped

2 tbs medium curry powder

750 g/1½ lb lean turkey, cut into cubes

200 ml/7 fl oz chicken stock

1 tbs garam masala

1 tbs chopped fresh coriander leaves

Heat the oil, and fry the onion over a medium heat until soft. Add the garlic, and fry for a few seconds more. Stir in the curry powder, and add the turkey. Raise the heat, and fry briskly for another 5 minutes. Add the stock, and simmer for about 10 minutes more, by which time the turkey should be done – test by cutting into a piece. Stir in the garam masala and the coriander, and serve with plain boiled rice.

Preparation time

5 minutes

Cooking time

15 minutes

Serves 4

RABBIT AND ONIONS

INGREDIENTS

2 tbs olive oil

750 g/1½ lb rabbit, cut in pieces

2 medium onions, finely chopped

3 or 4 tomatoes, skinned and chopped

1 tbs chopped fresh parsley

salt and pepper

175 ml/6 fl oz dry white wine or dry cider

Heat the oil in a flameproof casserole, add the rabbit pieces, and brown them on all sides. Add the onions, tomatoes, parsley, and salt and pepper. Add the wine or cider, cover, and simmer for about 15 minutes.

Preparation time

10 minutes

Cooking time

20 minutes

Serves 4

FAST WORK – SLOW COOKING

Many of the recipes in this section take at least an hour to cook – on the other hand, the preparation time is minimal. In the case of the casserole recipes, once they are ready to cook, you can put them in the oven and forget about them for an hour. If you are not ready when they are, you can switch off the oven, and leave the casserole in it to keep warm.

Marinating is a wonderful way to tenderize and add flavour to chicken and fish. It is also a good way of preparing dishes, with the minimum of effort, which can then be cooked very quickly. You can make the marinade quickly, and leave your fish or chicken sitting in it for as little as half an hour, or as long as overnight, until you are ready to cook it.

BRAISED CHICKEN

Preparation time

10 minutes

Cooking time

1 hour

Serves 4

Heat the oven to 190°C/375°F/gas 5. Heat the oil in a large casserole, and fry the bacon in it until the fat runs. Add the onions and mushrooms, and fry for 2 minutes, then remove with a slotted spoon. Put the chicken in the casserole, and brown it all over. Return the bacon, onions and mushrooms to the casserole. Sprinkle with the *herbes de Provence*, season, pour in the wine, and heat until the liquid bubbles. Then seal the casserole with a piece of foil under the lid, and put it in the oven for 1 hour. If you want a complete, one-dish meal, add tiny new potatoes about 20 minutes before the end of the cooking time.

INGREDIENTS

2 tbs cooking oil

4 rashers of smoked streaky bacon, diced

2 medium onions, finely chopped

1 chicken, weighing approx. 1.5 kg/3 lbs

a pinch of dried *herbes de Provence*

salt and pepper

1 large glass dry white wine

25 g/4 oz mushrooms, cleaned and sliced

MEDITERRANEAN CHICKEN

INGREDIENTS

2 tbs olive oil

1 red pepper and 1 yellow pepper, cleaned, with ribs and seeds removed, and finely sliced

1 medium onion, finely sliced

1 clove garlic, chopped

1 chicken, weighing approx. 1.5 kg/3 lb

150 ml/¼ pt chicken stock

a handful of black olives, preferably stoned

a sprig of thyme

salt and pepper

Heat the oven to 190°C/375°F/gas 5. Heat the oil in a casserole, and add the peppers, onion, and garlic. Lower the heat, and cook for 5 minutes, stirring from time to time. Remove with a slotted spoon, and reserve. Brown the chicken on all sides in the casserole. Return the peppers, onion, and garlic to the casserole. Add the stock, olives, thyme, and seasoning. Seal the casserole with a piece of foil, and put in the oven for about an hour.

Preparation time

10 minutes

Cooking time

1 hour

Serves 4

CHICKEN IN LEMON AND THYME MARINADE

INGREDIENTS

8 chicken drumsticks

125 ml/4 fl oz olive oil

juice of 2 lemons

2 cloves garlic, finely chopped

a sprig of fresh thyme

salt and freshly ground black pepper

Make up the marinade by combining all the ingredients in a dish, and put the chicken drumsticks in it for at least an hour – you can leave them in it overnight, in the refrigerator, if you wish.

When you are ready to cook the drumsticks, heat the grill to maximum, and grill them for about 5 minutes on each side, basting them with the marinade.

Preparation time

5 minutes

Marinating time

1 hour

Cooking time

10 minutes

Serves 4

SPICED INDIAN CHICKEN

Preparation time

5 minutes

Marinating time

1 hour

Cooking time

15 minutes

Serves 4

Put the chicken in a shallow dish. Mix all the marinade ingredients in a bowl, and pour over the chicken. Cover with clingfilm, and leave to marinate for at least an hour – however, you can leave it for up to a day in the refrigerator.

When you are ready to cook, heat the grill to maximum. Remove the chicken from the marinade, scraping any surplus back into the bowl. Grill the chicken for about 15 minutes, turning the pieces frequently, and basting them from time to time with a little of the marinade. Serve with *Tsatsiki* (Greek yogurt and cucumber salad), and with plain or spiced rice.

INGREDIENTS

4 chicken breasts, skinned, or 8 chicken drumsticks

150 ml/¼ pt plain yogurt

2 cloves garlic, crushed

1 or 2 tsp mild chilli powder

1 tsp ground coriander

a good pinch of salt

2 tbs oil

1 tbs lemon juice

To serve:

Tsatsiki

rice

CHICKEN IN CHABLIS

Preparation time

10 minutes

Cooking time

1 hr 10 minutes

Serves 4

Heat the oven to 175°C/350°F/gas 4. Mix together the flour, salt, and pepper, and coat the chicken breasts with this. Heat the oil in a pan, and fry the chicken breasts until they are brown on both sides. Remove the chicken to an ovenproof casserole. Stir the rest of the seasoned flour into the oil, and mix well. Add the tomatoes and white wine, and bring to the boil. Add the mushrooms and garlic. Pour this sauce over the chicken, cover, and put in the oven for 1 hour.

INGREDIENTS

125 g/4 oz wholewheat flour

2 tsp salt

1 tsp freshly ground black pepper

4 chicken breasts, skinned

4 tbs olive oil

250 g/8 oz can tomatoes

375 ml/12 fl oz Chablis, or other dry white wine

5 or 6 mushrooms, cleaned and sliced

2 cloves garlic, chopped

CHICKEN WITH THYME AND LEMON

INGREDIENTS

3 tbs wholemeal flour

2 tsp dried thyme

salt and freshly ground black pepper

8 chicken thighs

100 ml/3 fl oz milk

4 tbs oil

juice of 1 lemon

Heat the oven to 190°C/375°F/gas 5. Mix together the flour, thyme, and seasoning. Dip the chicken pieces in the milk, then coat them thoroughly with the flour mixture. Heat the oil in a frying pan, and fry the chicken on all sides, until it is golden brown. Transfer to a wire rack placed over a baking sheet. Pour the lemon juice over the chicken pieces, and bake them in the oven for 15 minutes. Serve either hot or cold.

Preparation time

5 minutes

Cooking time

30 minutes

Serves 4

DAUBE OF BEEF WITH TOMATO AND OLIVES

INGREDIENTS

3 tbs sunflower oil

750 g/1½ lbs beef rump, cut into 5 cm/2 in cubes

2 onions, sliced

1 tbs plain flour

300 ml/½ pt white wine

300 ml/½ pt beef stock

250 g/8 oz tomatoes, chopped

2 garlic cloves, crushed

1 *bouquet garni*

pared rind of 1 orange

salt and pepper

50 g/2 oz stoned green olives

50 g/2 oz stoned black olives

This dish is quick to prepare, and even better if it is cooked the day before, and reheated until piping hot. The same recipe can also be made using boned shoulder of lamb, which should be cooked for 1½ to 2 hours.

Heat the oil in a casserole, and add the beef, a little at a time, and brown it on all sides. Remove the beef with a slotted spoon. Add the onions, and sauté for 2 to 3 minutes. Sprinkle the flour over the onions, and – stirring continuously – allow them to brown. Gradually stir in the wine and stock to make a smooth sauce, and add the tomatoes, garlic, *bouquet garni*, orange rind, and seasoning. Bring to the boil to thicken the sauce, and return the meat to the casserole. Cover, and simmer very gently for 2½ hours.

Ten minutes before the end of cooking, discard the orange rind and the *bouquet garni*. Blanch the olives in boiling water to remove some of the salt, and add them to the casserole. Season to taste. Serve with potatoes mashed with olive oil and plenty of nutmeg.

Preparation time

10 minutes

Cooking time

3 hours

Serves 4

HEARTY IRISH STEW

Preparation time

10–15 minutes

Cooking time

1 hour

Serves 4

This casserole is better still if you prepare it with a good chicken stock, made from the bones of a roast. You could also add some other vegetables – turnips, Jerusalem artichokes, a few peas – just before the end of the cooking time. And instead of putting potatoes in the stew, you could bake them at the same time – use smallish, whole potatoes if you do this, scrub them, and prick them with a fork.

Heat the oven to 175°C/350°F/gas 4. Clean the lamb, and trim off the surplus fat. Dust the pieces of meat in the flour seasoned with the herbs and salt and pepper. Heat the oil in a hob-to-oven casserole, fry the onion gently for a minute or two, add the garlic, fry for another minute, then remove with a slotted spoon. Brown the pieces of lamb, return the onion and garlic to the casserole, and add the stock, carrots, potatoes, and thyme. Seal the casserole with foil, cover, and put it in the oven for 1 hour.

INGREDIENTS

1 kg/2 lbs best end of neck of lamb, cut into small pieces
2 tbs flour
mixed dried herbs
salt and freshly ground black pepper
3 tbs olive oil
1 large onion, chopped
3 cloves garlic, chopped
300 ml/½ pt vegetable stock
2 large carrots, washed, and cut into big chunks
2 large potatoes, washed, and cut into big chunks
a sprig of fresh thyme
1 tbs fresh parsley, chopped

MARINATED SARDINES WITH GRILLED CHICORY

Preparation time

5 minutes

Marinating time

1 hour

Cooking time

10 minutes

Serves 4

The sardines can be grilled after just an hour in the marinade, but the longer you leave them – all day or even overnight – the better the flavour will be.

Sprinkle the sardines with the oil. Mix together the garlic, shallots, lemon juice, and thyme, and smear this over the sardines. Leave to marinate.

When you are ready to cook the sardines, heat the grill. Halve each bulb of chicory or head of radicchio lengthways, and dip in the marinade. Grill for 3 minutes on each side. Grill the sardines for 2 minutes on each side. Serve with wedges of lime or lemon.

INGREDIENTS

8 sardines, gutted and scaled
4 tbs olive oil
1 clove garlic, crushed
2 shallots, finely chopped
2 tbs lemon juice
1 tbs fresh thyme
4 bulbs chicory or 1 head radicchio

GRAINS AND PULSES

BULGUR WITH AUBERGINES, ALMONDS, AND RAISINS

INGREDIENTS

125 g/4 oz bulgur or cracked wheat
4–6 tbs olive oil
1 large onion, thinly sliced
1 large aubergine, cut into cubes
2 tsp ground coriander
2 tsp ground cumin
75g/3 oz flaked almonds
50 g/2 oz raisins
salt and freshly ground black pepper

This recipe makes enough for at least 2 servings, but if some is left over it is just as good served cold. With chopped flat-leaved parsley added, it makes an excellent tabbouleh to serve at barbecues.

Simmer the bulgur wheat in twice its volume of water for 10 minutes, or until most or all of the water has been absorbed, and the grains are soft. Drain if necessary. Meanwhile, heat a little oil, and fry the onion until it turns brown. Add the aubergine and, stirring frequently, sauté until it is brown – you might need to add a little extra oil, since the aubergine acts like a sponge. Add the spices to the pan, and cook for 1 minute, stirring constantly. Lower the heat, and add the flaked almonds and raisins, and brown lightly. Stir the cooked bulgur wheat into the vegetables, season with salt and pepper, add extra oil, and sauté for 1 minute to heat through. Serve immediately.

Preparation time

5 minutes

Cooking time

15 minutes

Serves 2

BULGUR RISOTTO

INGREDIENTS

125 g/4 oz butter
1 onion, finely chopped
1 clove garlic, finely chopped
250 g/8 oz bulgur, washed and drained
450 ml/¾ pt good chicken or vegetable stock
good pinch of sea salt
To serve:
1 onion, finely sliced
1 tbs olive oil
125 ml/4 fl oz plain yogurt

This simple and satisfying risotto from the Middle East, traditionally served with creamy plain yogurt and fried onions, and a green salad, is a perfect main meal. You can also serve the risotto as an alternative to plain rice to accompany stews or goulashes.

Melt the butter in a non-stick pan, and sauté the onion and garlic until they are just changing colour. Add the bulgur, and stir over a low heat until it glistens with the butter. Then add the stock – enough to cover it by a good inch (approx. 2.5 cm). Bring to the boil, add the salt, cover the pan, lower the heat, and cook for another 10 minutes, by which time the bulgur should be cooked, and all the stock absorbed. If it dries out before the bulgur is cooked, add more stock as necessary. Meanwhile, fry the onion until it is almost crisp in the olive oil. When the bulgur is ready, serve it with the fried onions and yogurt as a garnish.

Preparation time

5 minutes

Cooking time

20 minutes

Serves 4

BEAN CASSEROLE

Preparation time

15 minutes

Cooking time

20 minutes

Serves 4-6

Heat the oil, and fry the onion and garlic for 2 or 3 minutes. Add the chilli, mustard, and vinegar, and simmer for 1 minute. Stir in the tomato purée, Worcestershire sauce, tomatoes, and stock. Season to taste with salt and pepper. Add the swede, carrots, and parsnips, and simmer for 20 minutes until tender – top up with more water if necessary. Add the mushrooms, chickpeas, and beans, and cook for another 5 minutes. Sprinkle with the parsley, and serve.

INGREDIENTS

1 tbs olive oil

1 onion, sliced

2 cloves garlic, crushed

1 tsp chilli powder

a pinch of English mustard powder

2 tbs cider vinegar

1 tbs tomato purée

a dash of Worcestershire sauce

1 small can chopped tomatoes

300 ml/½pt vegetable stock

salt and freshly ground black pepper

1 small swede, diced

375 g/12 oz carrots, sliced

375 g/12 oz parsnips, sliced

125 g/4 oz button mushrooms, sliced

1 can chickpeas, drained and rinsed

1 small can borlotti beans, drained and rinsed

4 tbs chopped fresh parsley

MILLET RISOTTO

INGREDIENTS

2 tbs extra-virgin olive oil

1 medium onion, chopped

1 clove garlic, chopped

250 g/8 oz millet

1 green pepper, diced

900 ml/1½ pt vegetable stock

2 tsp yeast extract

1 bay leaf

1 bouquet garni

salt and pepper

250 g/8 oz mushrooms, sliced

In a large, thick-bottomed saucepan, heat the oil, add the onion, and stir until it is soft. Add the garlic, stir for another minute, add the millet, and stir vigorously for 2 minutes. Add the green pepper, and stir for another 2 minutes. Then add the stock, yeast extract, herbs, and salt and pepper. Bring to the boil, and simmer gently for 15 minutes, covered – do not stir while it is simmering. Add the mushrooms, stir thoroughly, and cook for another 5 minutes.

Preparation time

5 minutes

Cooking time

25–30 minutes

Serves 4

INSTANT CHICKPEA CASSEROLE

INGREDIENTS

4 tbs vegetable oil

1 large onion, finely chopped

3 cloves garlic, chopped

1 can chopped tomatoes

1 can chickpeas, rinsed and drained

500 g/1 lb frozen mixed vegetables

1 *bouquet garni*

900 ml/1½ pt vegetable stock

salt and pepper

2 tbs chopped fresh parsley

Heat the oil in a large, thick-bottomed saucepan. Add the onion, and cook until it is just soft. Add the garlic, and cook for another 2 minutes. Add the tomatoes with their juice, and bring to the boil. Add the chickpeas, frozen vegetables, *bouquet garni*, stock, and seasoning. Cover, and simmer for 15 minutes. Place in bowls, sprinkle with the parsley, and serve.

Preparation time

5 minutes

Cooking time

25 minutes

Serves 4

RED HOT RICE

Preparation time

10 minutes

Cooking time

25 minutes

Serves 4

Boil a pan of water, and cook the rice – it will take 20–25 minutes. You can use boil-in-the-bag or easy-cook rice. Meanwhile, wash the pepper, remove the ribs and seeds, and slice it into small strips. Wash, slit open, and deseed the chilli – rinse your hands carefully afterwards. Heat the oil, and gently sauté the chilli in it for 5 minutes, then fish it out, and discard it. Add the onion, garlic, and red pepper, and sauté them over a low heat until they are soft. When the rice is cooked, put it in a salad bowl, pour in the contents of the frying pan, and stir through.

INGREDIENTS

125 g/4 oz boil-in-the-bag brown rice

1 small red pepper

1 small, fresh red chilli

3 tbs vegetable oil

1 medium onion, finely sliced

2 cloves garlic, finely sliced

SUN-DRIED TOMATO RISOTTO

Preparation time

5 minutes

Cooking time

40 minutes

Serves 4

Heat the oil, and fry the onion and garlic for 2 to 3 minutes. Add the rice, sun-dried tomatoes – drain them first if they are in oil – stock, and fresh tomatoes. Bring to the boil, season to taste, and simmer for approximately 40 minutes. Add the basil, and stir in the cheese before serving.

NOTE: For a quicker version of this recipe, you can use boil-in-the-bag or easy-cook brown rice. While it's cooking according to the manufacturer's instructions, heat the oil, and fry the onion and garlic until they are just changing colour. Add the sun-dried and fresh tomatoes, and sauté for another 5 minutes. When the rice is ready, stir it into the tomato mixture, season to taste, add the basil, stir in the cheese, and serve.

INGREDIENTS

2 tbs vegetable oil

1 medium onion, chopped

2 cloves garlic, chopped

250 g/8 oz brown rice

175 g/6 oz sun-dried tomatoes, chopped

750 ml/1¼ pt vegetable stock

4 ripe red tomatoes, peeled and chopped

salt and freshly ground black pepper

1 tbs fresh basil, cut up

2 tbs grated Cheddar, Parmesan, or other hard cheese

BUCKWHEAT WITH MUSHROOMS AND ONIONS

INGREDIENTS

250 g/8 oz buckwheat
1 egg
50 g/2 oz butter
450 ml/¾ pt boiling water
1 tbs extra-virgin olive oil
1 large onion, coarsely chopped
250 g/8 oz mushrooms, sliced
salt and freshly ground black pepper
1 tbs chopped fresh parsley
To serve:
125 ml/4 fl oz plain low-fat yogurt

First cook the buckwheat: beat the egg in a bowl, add the buckwheat, mix thoroughly, and cook the mixture in a non-stick pan with no oil until it is toasted and dry. Grease a casserole dish with some of the butter. Add the buckwheat, the rest of the butter, a pinch of salt, and the boiling water, and cook in a preheated oven, 175°C/350°F/gas 4, for 20 minutes.

While the buckwheat is cooking, heat the oil in a frying pan, add the onion, and cook until it is soft. Add the mushrooms, and cook for another 5 minutes. Season with salt and pepper, and add the parsley, stirring continuously. When the buckwheat is cooked, add the onion and mushrooms, stir thoroughly, and serve with the yogurt as an accompaniment.

Preparation time

5 minutes

Cooking time

25 minutes

Serves 4

PASTA

Pasta is one of the original fast foods, uniquely satisfying, tasty, and versatile. Many of the classic pasta dishes of Italy take no more than 15 minutes to prepare from start to finish, and once you're familiar with the technique, you can throw together an appetizing meal from store cupboard ingredients in no time. If you want your pasta to be as good as almost anything dished up in a real Italian *trattoria*, there are a few vital rules:

1. The pasta must be made from 100 per cent durum wheat. Some supermarket pastas are made with mixtures of different flours, and produce a flabby, disappointing dish, however delicious the sauce may be. If possible, buy Italian-made pasta.

2. Pasta must be cooked in large quantities of well-salted water, so that it starts to cook evenly the second it's lowered in, and doesn't stick.

3. Pasta must be cooked only to the point where it still has a little bite – the stage known as *al dente*. If it's completely soft, you may as well throw it away.

4. Pasta continues cooking after it has been removed from the water, so it must never be kept hanging around. Once it is cooked, and the sauce added, it should be served without delay.

SALMON, MUSHROOM, AND CREAM SAUCE

Preparation time

10 minutes

Cooking time

10 minutes

Serves 4

Remove the bones from the salmon. Clean and chop the mushrooms, and put the salmon and mushrooms in a saucepan with the cream and white wine. Crumble in the stock cube, and add the sweetcorn. Simmer for 5 minutes, and at the last moment add the fresh herbs. This sauce is particularly good served with tagliatelle.

INGREDIENTS

225 g/7 oz canned salmon
6–8 mushrooms
150 ml/¼ pt double cream
75 ml/2 fl oz white wine
½ vegetable stock cube
1 tbs sweetcorn
2 tbs chopped fresh mint, basil, or parsley

MARLENE'S TUNA PASTA

INGREDIENTS

225 g/7 oz tuna, canned in oil
400 g/14 oz can Italian peeled tomatoes
3 cloves garlic
1 medium onion, finely chopped
200 ml/7 fl oz single cream
salt and a little dried chilli – or cayenne pepper – to taste
1 tsp capers
a few leaves of fresh basil
1 tbs olive oil
1 tbs salt
600 g/1¼ lb pasta

This recipe comes from The New School Cookbook, *a compilation of recipes contributed by parents, staff, and pupils at the International School in Rome. This recipe came from Marlene Nijhof. A variation on an Italian theme, it is a real store cupboard invention that goes well with pasta shells. The cream counters the dryness that some tuna sauces have.*

Put a large pan of water on to boil. Put the drained tuna, tomatoes, garlic, onion, cream, chilli, capers, and basil into a food processor. Let it run for under a minute, or until you have a rough-textured sauce – it shouldn't be too smooth. Tip the mixture into a small pan, and heat very gently over a low heat. When the pasta water boils, add the oil and salt. Put in the pasta, and cook until just *al dente*. Strain the pasta, tip it into a large hot dish, stir in the sauce, and serve.

Preparation time

10 minutes

Cooking time

10–15 minutes

Serves 6

TUNA AND BLACK OLIVE SAUCE

INGREDIENTS

Tomato sauce from Presia's Eggs Bolognese (p.84)
200 g/7 oz tuna, canned in oil
8–10 stoned black olives
250 g/8 oz pasta of your choice

Make the tomato sauce, as in the recipe for Presia's Eggs Bolognese, omitting the potatoes and the eggs. Add the tuna, drained of its oil, and the olives. Season to taste, and heat through. Meanwhile cook the pasta: when it is *al dente*, strain, stir in the sauce, and serve.

Preparation time

10 minutes

Cooking time

15–20 minutes

Serves 4

MEATBALL AND TOMATO SAUCE

Preparation time

5 minutes

Cooking time

20 minutes

Serves 4

This is an American-style recipe that turns spaghetti into a substantial meal.

Mix together the mincemeat, garlic, fresh herbs, and salt and pepper. Break the egg into it, and mix it up with your hands. Form the mixture into meatballs the size of table-tennis balls. Heat the oil in a frying pan, and fry the meatballs gently for 7–10 minutes. When they are cooked through, add them to the tomato sauce, and serve with spaghetti, cooked *al dente*.

INGREDIENTS
500 g/1 lb minced beef
3 cloves garlic, chopped
2 tbs chopped fresh mint and parsley
salt and black pepper
1 egg
2 tbs olive oil
tomato sauce as in preceding recipe

SPAGHETTI WITH PESTO AND VEGETABLES

Preparation time

10 minutes

Cooking time

12–15 minutes

Serves 4

To prepare the sauce, you can use ready-made pesto, available in jars.

Heat a large pan of water. When it boils add the salt, and plunge in the spaghetti and the vegetables. By the time the pasta is cooked *al dente*, the vegetables should be just tender. Just before you drain the spaghetti, take a tablespoonful of the cooking water, and stir it into the pesto. Drain the pasta and vegetables, and quickly transfer them to a hot dish. Stir in the pesto, and toss. Garnish with the basil leaves, and serve. Have a little grated Parmesan cheese ready for those who want it.

INGREDIENTS
1 tbs salt
300 g/10 oz spaghetti
50 g/2 oz French beans, cleaned and finely chopped
50 g/2 oz new potatoes, peeled and finely diced
50 g/2 oz courgettes, cleaned and diced
2 or 3 tbs pesto sauce
To serve:
a few fresh basil leaves
Parmesan cheese, grated

COURGETTE PASTA

INGREDIENTS

| 1 small fresh courgette |
| a knob of butter |
| 1 tbs freshly grated Parmesan cheese |
| a little vegetable oil |
| 1 tbs salt |
| 100 g/3½ oz pasta – preferably spaghettini |
| freshly ground black pepper |

A fresh, light pasta for early summer, when the first small, tender courgettes appear in the shops. Speed and a hot serving dish are vital to the success of this pasta.

Put a large pan of water on to boil. Have ready to hand the courgette, washed and dried, the butter, the Parmesan, and a grater. When the water boils, add a little oil, the salt, and the pasta. Grate the courgette using the finest side of the grater. When the pasta is cooked, drain it, and quickly tip it into the hot dish. Add the courgette immediately to the pasta, stir in the butter and Parmesan cheese, season with salt and pepper, and toss. Eat at once.

Preparation time

5 minutes

Cooking time

15 minutes

Serves 1

CAULIFLOWER CARBONARA

INGREDIENTS

| 250 g/8 oz spaghetti – use a mixture of white and green |
| 1 small cauliflower, cut into tiny florets |
| 2 tbs extra-virgin olive oil |
| 1 onion, finely chopped |
| 4 tbs dry white wine |
| 2 eggs, beaten |
| 2 tbs grated Parmesan cheese |
| 1 or 2 tbs chopped fresh basil or tarragon |
| freshly ground black pepper |
| *To garnish:* |
| a sprig of fresh basil |
| a few olives |

Bring a large pan of water to the boil, add one tablespoonful of salt, and put the pasta in to cook. While it is cooking, blanch the cauliflower in boiling water for 2 minutes, and drain. Heat the oil in a large pan. Sauté the onion until it is soft. Add the cauliflower and wine and keep hot. Mix together the eggs, cheese, herbs, and pepper. As soon as the spaghetti is cooked *al dente*, drain, add to the pan with the cauliflower, and carefully pour in the egg mixture, stirring all the time over a very gentle heat. Heat through until the egg scrambles. Garnish with the basil and olives, and serve.

Preparation time

5 minutes

Cooking time

20 minutes

Serves 4

PASTA WITH BROCCOLI

Preparation time

10 minutes

Cooking time

10–15 minutes

Serves 4

For this dish, you need little florets of broccoli – or a mixture of broccoli and cauliflower florets – together with some of the stems, finely chopped. Keep the thick stems for another dish.

Heat a large pan of salted water for the pasta. When it boils, add the broccoli – or broccoli and cauliflower mixture – and cook for about 5 minutes. The vegetables should still be *al dente*. Remove from the water with a slotted spoon, and put aside. Bring the water back to the boil, and add the pasta.

While the pasta is cooking, heat the oil in a large frying pan, and add the garlic, the anchovy paste (note that a little goes a long way) and the chilli. Add the cooked vegetables, sprinkle with pepper, and toss for 4 or 5 minutes. Keep the mixture hot until the pasta is ready – the lovely warm flavours will continue to be released into the hot oil. When it is cooked *al dente*, drain the pasta, put it in a hot dish, and add the broccoli and the flavoured oil. Toss together, and serve with the Parmesan cheese.

INGREDIENTS
375 g/12 oz broccoli – or broccoli and cauliflower – florets
375 g/12 oz pasta
4 tbs olive oil
3 fat cloves garlic, finely chopped
a squeeze of anchovy paste from a tube
a good pinch of crushed dried chillies
freshly ground black pepper
3 tbs grated Parmesan cheese

TAGLIATELLE WITH GREEN SAUCE

Preparation time

10 minutes

Cooking time

10 minutes

Serves 4

Put the basil, parsley, mint, and pine nuts in a blender or food processor with 2 teaspoonfuls of the oil. Blend to a smooth paste. Add the rest of the oil, the *fromage frais*, and the Parmesan cheese, and blend again very briefly. Cook the pasta until it is just *al dente* in plenty of boiling salted water, drain it, turn it into a hot dish, stir in the green sauce, and serve.

INGREDIENTS
a good handful of fresh basil and parsley
a few leaves of mint
1 tbs pine nuts
75 ml/2 fl oz olive oil
50 g/2 oz *fromage frais*
125 g/4 oz Parmesan cheese, grated
500 g/1 lb tagliatelle verdi

VEGETABLE DISHES

SUPERFAST CABBAGE

INGREDIENTS

1 curly green cabbage

1 tbs butter

freshly ground black pepper

1 tbs grainy mustard

Thoroughly wash the cabbage, shred it, and put it in a pan with a couple of tablespoons of water. Cover the pan, and cook the cabbage over a low heat until is just *al dente* – it should be bright green, and still have plenty of bite to it. Drain the cabbage. In the same pan melt the butter, add a little pepper, and stir in the grainy mustard. Return the cabbage, and toss all of the ingredients together for a couple of minutes.

Preparation time

2–3 minutes

Cooking time

10 minutes

Serves 4

CABBAGE WITH ONION AND BACON

INGREDIENTS

1 medium cabbage

1 tbs vegetable oil

1 medium onion, coarsely chopped

3 or 4 rashers streaky bacon, cut in pieces

salt and pepper

Wash and shred the cabbage, but don't dry it. Heat the oil in a big saucepan, and gently fry the onion and bacon together until the onion is just changing colour, and the bacon is nearly crisp. Add the cabbage, salt and pepper, and stir. Put the lid on, turn down the heat, and simmer. Shake the pan, and give the contents a stir a couple of times – the cabbage will steam cook – until the cabbage is cooked just *al dente*.

Preparation time

5 minutes

Cooking time

10 minutes

Serves 4

SPICED RED CABBAGE

Preparation time

5 minutes

Cooking time

20 minutes

Serves 4

Wash and shred the cabbage, and put it in a pan with the apple, red wine vinegar, cloves, and salt and pepper. Sprinkle over 2 or 3 tablespoonfuls of water, add the brown sugar, cover, and simmer for 20 minutes.

INGREDIENTS
1 fairly small red cabbage
1 large cooking apple, peeled and sliced in segments
3 tbs red wine vinegar
10 cloves
salt and freshly ground black pepper
1 or 2 tsp brown sugar

POTATO GALETTE

Preparation time

10 minutes

Cooking time

15 minutes

Serves 4

Peel the potatoes, and grate them in a food processor. Turn into a bowl, and add the egg yolks, grated onion, parsley, and garlic, and mix. Crush the mixture into a thin cake, and dust with a little flour.

Heat enough oil in a frying pan to come about half way up the side of the cake. Add the potato cake, and fry it on both sides until it is golden brown. Turn out onto kitchen paper to blot up excess fat. Sprinkle with a little grated nutmeg, and serve.

INGREDIENTS
4 medium potatoes
2 egg yolks
1 medium onion, peeled and grated
3 tbs finely chopped fresh parsley
2 cloves garlic, finely chopped
a little plain flour or potato flour
sunflower or corn oil
a pinch of grated nutmeg

QUICK MASHED POTATOES

INGREDIENTS

500 g/1 lb potatoes

150 ml/¼ pt milk

a little sea salt

50 g/2 oz butter

a pinch of freshly ground pepper

a little fresh parsley, finely chopped

Peel the potatoes, and dice them very small. Put them in a pan with the milk and a touch of salt. Bring to the boil, lower the heat, cover, and simmer for 10–15 minutes until the potatoes are tender.

Mash with a potato masher – you may need to add a little more milk at this stage – and stir in the butter and pepper. Sprinkle with the parsley, and serve.

Preparation time

5 minutes

Cooking time

20 minutes

Serves 4

TURNIP AND POTATO CREAM

INGREDIENTS

500 g/1 lb small turnips

1 medium potato

3 tbs single cream

salt and pepper

a little fresh parsley, finely chopped

If the turnips are very young and tender they won't need peeling – just scrub them, and cut them into small dice. Scrub, and dice the potato. Put the vegetables in a pan with enough water to cover them. Bring to the boil, and simmer until they are tender – about 15 minutes. Drain off all but 1 tablespoon of cooking water, and mash the potatoes and turnips into this – it should be quite a rough consistency. Stir in the cream, season to taste with salt and pepper, and sprinkle with the parsley.

Preparation time

10 minutes

Cooking time

15 minutes

Serves 4

TURNIP PURÉE

Preparation time

5 minutes

Cooking time

20 minutes

Serves 4

Scrub the turnips, and cut them into quarters. Heat the milk in a pan, add the turnips, and steam cook them, covered, over a low heat until they are tender – about 15 minutes. Purée the turnips with a potato masher, stir in the butter, and sprinkle with the nutmeg.

INGREDIENTS

500 g/1 lb tender, young turnips

150 ml/¼ pt milk

50 g/2 oz butter

a pinch of grated nutmeg

FENNEL PARMIGIANA

Preparation time

5 minutes

Cooking time

20 minutes

Serves 4

Heat the oven to 200°C/400°F/gas 6. Clean and quarter the heads of fennel, and chop off the thick bottoms. Cook the fennel in a pan of boiling water until just tender – you should be able to push a sharp knife through easily. Drain well, butter an ovenproof dish, place the fennel in it, sprinkle with the Parmesan, and bake in the oven for 5 minutes.

INGREDIENTS

2 large heads or 3 medium-sized heads of fresh fennel

1 tbs butter

3 tbs grated Parmesan cheese

BRAISED FENNEL

INGREDIENTS

2 large or 4 small heads of fresh fennel
1 tbs olive oil
1 tbs chopped fresh parsley
a sprig of fresh thyme
6 peppercorns
a glass of dry white wine

Clean the fennel, and cut it into halves or quarters. Heat the oil in a shallow casserole, and fry the pieces of fennel until they are lightly browned. Add the parsley, thyme, and peppercorns, then pour in the wine, and let it bubble for a minute. Cover the dish, and cook over a very low heat for about 25 minutes.

Preparation time

10 minutes

Cooking time

30 minutes

Serves 4

SPINACH ITALIAN-STYLE

INGREDIENTS

1 kg/2 lb spinach
2 tbs olive oil
1 or 2 cloves garlic, chopped
1 fresh red or green chilli, chopped
a little fresh lemon juice

Italian greengrocers sell a wide range of greens, ready-trimmed and washed. As well as spinach, wild chicory, beetroot tops, and endives can all be cooked in the following way – and even mixed together. When cooking spinach, you don't have to trim off all the stalks – only the very toughest and thickest should be removed.

Wash the spinach thoroughly in several changes of water. Put it while it is still wet in a large pan, cover, and cook over the lowest possible heat. Within 10 minutes the greens will have wilted, and just become tender. Drain thoroughly.

At this point, you can choose 2 ways of serving the spinach. Either heat the oil in a big pan, quickly sauté the garlic and chilli, toss the spinach very quickly in the flavoured oil, and serve. Alternatively, you can dress the drained spinach with a little olive oil and freshly pressed lemon juice, and serve it lukewarm.

Preparation time

5 minutes

Cooking time

10 minutes

Serves 4

SPINACH AND YOGURT

Preparation time

5 minutes

Cooking time

10 minutes

Serves 2

This is the perfect vegetable dish for a light summer lunch. If possible make it with fresh, young spinach leaves – but frozen spinach will do.

Clean the spinach thoroughly, and put it in a pan – don't add water. Cover, and cook over a very low heat until it has wilted and turned soft – this will take about 10 minutes. Drain the spinach well – you can save the juice, and store it for a drink. When the spinach is cool, chop it roughly, and stir in the yogurt and sour cream. Season lightly, add the mint, and serve.

INGREDIENTS

500 g/1 lb fresh spinach, or 250 g/8 oz frozen leaf spinach

3 or 4 tbs plain yogurt

2 tbs sour cream

salt and pepper

2 or 3 sprigs fresh mint, chopped

FRENCH GREEN BEANS WITH TOMATOES

Preparation time

10 minutes

Cooking time

25 minutes

Serves 4

If using fresh beans, wash, and top and tail them. Cook the beans in boiling water until they are just *al dente*. Drain well. Heat the oil in the pan. Put in the beans, add the tomatoes, and toss together for a minute or two. Season to taste with salt and pepper, and serve.

INGREDIENTS

500 g/1 lb fresh or frozen French beans

1 tbs olive oil

3 red tomatoes, skinned and chopped

salt and freshly ground black pepper

CAULIFLOWER GRATIN I

INGREDIENTS

1 medium cauliflower

1 or 2 tbs butter

3 tbs grated Parmesan cheese

freshly ground pepper

This is a quicker, lighter version of that favourite old stand-by, cauliflower cheese.

Heat the oven to 200°C/400°F/gas 6. Wash the cauliflower, and separate the florets. Steam-cook these in a couple of inches (approx. 5 cm) of water in a covered pan until just *al dente*, and drain. Butter a shallow ovenproof dish, and sprinkle in a little of the Parmesan cheese. Add the cauliflower florets, and sprinkle the rest of the cheese over them. Melt 1 tablespoon of butter, pour it over, and put the dish in the oven for 10 minutes, or until the cauliflower is nicely browned.

Preparation time

10 minutes

Cooking time

15 minutes

Serves 4

CAULIFLOWER GRATIN II

INGREDIENTS

1 good, firm, medium cauliflower

3 or 4 cloves garlic, sliced finely

3 tbs olive oil

50 g/2 oz butter

salt and freshly ground pepper

2 tbs grated Parmesan cheese

Separate the cauliflower into florets, and steam them in a covered pan in 2 inches (5 cm) of water. Meanwhile, heat the oil and butter in a frying pan, and sauté the garlic until it is just changing colour. When the cauliflower is cooked *al dente*, pour over the oil, butter, and garlic from the frying pan, season with salt and pepper, and sprinkle with the grated Parmesan.

Preparation time

5 minutes

Cooking time

10 minutes

Serves 4

CAULIFLOWER WITH GARLIC AND CHILLI

Preparation time

5 minutes

Cooking time

10 minutes

Serves 4

Broccoli can be cooked the same way.

Wash the cauliflower, and separate it into small florets. Drain, and put them in a pan with 2 tablespoonfuls of water. Cover, and cook until tender, but still slightly *al dente*. Drain. Heat the oil in the same pan. Add the chilli and the garlic, and sauté for 1 minute. Add the cauliflower. Toss, and serve.

INGREDIENTS
1 cauliflower
2 tbs olive oil
1 dried red chilli, deseeded and chopped
1 clove garlic, chopped

SWEETCORN WITH PEPPERS

Preparation time

5 minutes

Cooking time

15 minutes

Serves 4

Prepare the sweetcorn. If you are using fresh it will need to be stripped from the cobs. You can prepare this dish using canned sweetcorn – choose a brand with no added sugar, and drain it well. It can also be made with frozen sweetcorn kernels – you will need to drop them for a minute into boiling water to defrost them, and drain them.

Heat the butter in a pan, add the onion and pepper, and sauté for 5 minutes. Add the sweetcorn. Season with salt, pepper, and paprika. Cover the pan, and simmer for 10 minutes.

INGREDIENTS
500 g/1 lb sweetcorn kernels
50 g/2 oz butter
1 medium onion, finely sliced
1 red and 1 green pepper, deseeded, deribbed, and sliced into strips
salt and pepper
a little paprika

PEAS WITH LETTUCE

INGREDIENTS

1 head of soft lettuce
500 g/1 lb peas – you can use frozen
a pinch of salt
25 g/1 oz butter

If you use frozen peas for this dish, blanch them quickly in boiling water to thaw them first, and drain them. Pull the leaves from the lettuce, and wash them carefully – but don't dry them. Cover the bottom of a non-stick saucepan with the lettuce leaves. Add the peas, salt, and the butter. Cover with another layer of lettuce leaves. Cover the pan, and cook over a very gentle heat for 10 minutes.

Preparation time

5 minutes

Cooking time

10 minutes

Serves 4

PEAS WITH BACON AND MINT

INGREDIENTS

500 g/1 lb peas
4 rashers streaky bacon, finely chopped
2 or 3 sprigs of fresh mint, chopped

Cook the peas until they are just tender. Fry the bacon until it is turning crisp. Pour off most of the fat, add the peas, toss them for a moment with the bacon, and add the chopped mint.

Preparation time

5 minutes

Cooking time

10 minutes

Serves 4

AROMATIC MUSHROOMS

Preparation time

5 minutes

Cooking time

25 minutes

Serves 4

Serve these mushrooms with plain rice, or Bulgur Risotto (see page 115), and a green salad.

Clean the mushrooms, and slice them thinly. Warm the olive oil in a pan. Add the garlic slices, bay leaf, coriander seeds, and seasoning. Add the mushrooms, and cover the pan. Shake gently, and cook over a very low heat for 20 minutes. Remove the bay leaf before serving the mushrooms.

INGREDIENTS
500 g/1 lb small white, or flat field mushrooms
3 tbs olive oil
2 cloves garlic, sliced in half
1 bay leaf
6–8 coriander seeds
salt and freshly ground black pepper

ITALIAN VEGETABLE GRILL

Preparation time

20 minutes

Cooking time

20 minutes

Serves 4

Heat the grill to maximum. Halve the courgettes lengthways. Cut the aubergine into wide, flat strips lengthways. Halve the peppers, remove the ribs and seeds, and cut them into wide, flat strips. Line the grill pan with foil. Put in the sliced vegetables and the mushroom, and brush them with a little olive oil. Grill for 2 to 3 minutes. Turn them over, and grill for a further 3 minutes.

Arrange the lettuce leaves on a heat-proof plate. Place the mushroom in the middle, and arrange the grilled vegetables around it. In a bowl, stir the garlic into 2 tablespoonfuls of olive oil, season with salt and pepper, and dribble this dressing over the vegetables. Slice the mozzarella into 4, put the slices on top of the mushroom, and return to the grill for a minute – or just long enough for the cheese to melt. Serve with thick chunks of bread.

INGREDIENTS
4 small courgettes
1 aubergine
1 red and 1 yellow pepper
1 large field mushroom
2 or 3 tbs olive oil
lettuce leaves
2 cloves garlic, finely chopped
salt and pepper
125 g/4 oz mozzarella cheese

GRILLED TOMATOES

INGREDIENTS

4 big, ripe beef tomatoes

a sprinkling of dried *fines herbes* or oregano

2 tbs grated Parmesan cheese

Heat the grill. Halve the tomatoes, and grill for about 5 minutes. Sprinkle them with the herbs and grated Parmesan cheese, and return to the grill for another minute or two until the cheese has melted.

Preparation time

5 minutes

Cooking time

10 minutes

Serves 4

PIQUANT BEETROOT

INGREDIENTS

1 medium-sized cooked beetroot

25 g/1 oz butter

1 tsp Dijon mustard

1 tbs soured cream

1 tbs chopped parsley or chives

Peel and cube the beetroot. Heat the butter in a pan, toss the beetroot in it over a gentle heat until it has warmed through. Take it out with a slotted spoon, and put it in a warmed dish. Add the mustard to the buttery juices in the pan, and mix. Stir in the cream. Pour over the beetroot, and sprinkle with the parsley or chives.

Preparation time

5 minutes

Cooking time

10 minutes

Serves 2

SALADS

Most of the Superfast Food salads are so substantial that, served with a crusty wholewheat roll and a piece of fruit, they are almost satisfying meals in themselves. You will also find some lighter, classic salads, included for their nutritious green leaves and fresh, sharp flavour.

Although pre-washed supermarket salad packs are a good stand-by when you're in a rush, a salad that you wash and prepare yourself has the advantage of being much fresher and richer in vitamins. A salad-spinner is an essential gadget in the Superfast Food kitchen, since it makes such quick work of drying salad leaves.

Make a supply of good French Dressing *(see page 143)* – you can keep it stored in a tightly sealed jar or bottle, in a cool, dark place.

DUTCH SALAD

Preparation time

10 minutes

Cooking time

10 minutes

Serves 4

Wash the potatoes, and put them in a panful of boiling water until they are cooked, then dice them. Slice the hard-boiled eggs. Wash and dice the apples. Chop the herrings into bite-sized pieces. Peel and dice the beetroot. Slice the cucumbers.

Make a ring of diced beetroot around the edge of the salad bowl, and pile the potatoes, apples, herrings, and cucumbers into the middle of the beetroot ring. Top with the egg slices. Make a dressing with the yogurt, oil, garlic, and salt and pepper, and pour over the salad. Garnish with a sprinkling of parsley.

INGREDIENTS

6–8 tiny new potatoes

4 eggs, hard-boiled

2 medium-sized apples

4 rollmop herrings

2 medium-sized beetroot

2 pickled dill cucumbers

For the dressing:

125 ml/4 fl oz natural yogurt

1 tbs olive oil

1 clove garlic, chopped

salt and pepper

1 tbs finely chopped fresh parsley

SALADE NIÇOISE

INGREDIENTS

1 crisp lettuce

2 eggs, hard-boiled and halved

4 firm, red tomatoes, quartered

½ cucumber, finely sliced

a handful of radishes, washed

12 black olives

For the dressing:

3 tbs extra-virgin olive oil

2 tsp white wine vinegar

a good pinch of dried oregano

salt and pepper

some fresh herbs, chopped

There is no hard-and-fast recipe for this classic salad. You can turn it into a complete meal by adding extra eggs, a can of tuna or anchovies, or even a few prawns. If you have any cooked green beans left over, or boiled new potatoes, add those too.

Wash and dry the lettuce, and arrange it in a salad bowl. Add the eggs, tomatoes, cucumber, radishes, and olives.

Mix together the oil, vinegar, and oregano, and season with salt and pepper to taste. Pour the dressing over the salad, and toss very lightly. Garnish with the fresh herbs.

Preparation time

10 minutes

Cooking time

10 minutes

Serves 4

BREAD AND TOMATO SALAD

INGREDIENTS

4 slices of bread

3 or 4 tbs extra-virgin olive oil

2 cloves garlic, finely chopped

3 or 4 plump, ripe tomatoes, roughly chopped

1 tbs fresh lemon juice

sea salt and freshly ground black pepper

2 tbs chopped fresh basil, chives, or parsley

This is a lovely, rich salad, full of Mediterranean sunshine. Use only the freshest, deep-red tomatoes with plenty of flavour, and a good-quality grainy bread – perhaps one of the speciality breads to be found in good supermarkets.

Remove the crusts, and cut the bread slices into cubes. Heat the oil in a frying pan, add the bread and garlic, and toss until all the oil is absorbed, and the bread is beginning to turn crisp. Put the bread into a salad bowl, add the tomatoes, lemon juice, a little salt and plenty of pepper, and the herbs. Toss all the ingredients together.

Preparation time

15 minutes

Serves 1

BIBI'S CRAB, CHEESE, AND BACON SALAD

This is a versatile salad. You can vary it by adding a diced avocado, and by using tuna instead of crab meat, if you prefer.

Preparation time

10 minutes

Cooking time

3–4 minutes

Serves 4

Wash, dry, and tear up the iceberg lettuce into pieces. Add the grated cheese, crab meat, mayonnaise, and grated carrot. Chop up the bacon, fry it until it is crispy, drain it on kitchen paper, and add it to the other ingredients. Make the dressing by combining the remaining ingredients, pour over the salad, and toss everything together.

INGREDIENTS

1 small or ½ large Iceberg lettuce
3 tbs grated Cheddar cheese
250 g/8 oz cooked crab meat
2 tbs mayonnaise
2 large carrots, finely grated
4 rashers streaky bacon
For the dressing:
2 tbs olive oil
2 tsp lemon juice
salt and freshly ground pepper
a pinch of cayenne pepper

WATERCRESS, AVOCADO, AND BACON SALAD

Wash, trim, and dry the watercress, and arrange it in a salad bowl. Peel, stone, and slice the avocado, and add it to the bowl. Chop the streaky bacon, heat the oil, and fry the bacon pieces until they are crisp. Add the vinegar to the pan, season with salt and pepper, and pour over the salad.

Preparation time

10 minutes

Cooking time

3 minutes

Serves 2

INGREDIENTS

a bunch of watercress
1 avocado
2 slices streaky bacon
1 tbs olive oil
1 tsp vinegar
a little salt and freshly ground pepper

SPINACH, MUSHROOM, SUNFLOWER SEED, AND BACON SALAD

INGREDIENTS

250 g/8 oz young, tender spinach leaves
175 g/6 oz mushrooms
4 rashers streaky bacon
2 tbs olive oil
1 tbs sunflower seeds
2 tsp vinegar
salt and a little freshly ground black pepper

Wash and dry the spinach leaves, and arrange them in a salad bowl. Wipe and slice the mushrooms, and add them to the bowl. Chop the bacon, and fry it in a non-stick pan until it is crispy. Remove the bacon pieces with a slotted spoon, and add them to the salad. Put the olive oil in the pan, heat it, and add the sunflower seeds. Toss them until they are lightly browned. Add the vinegar, season with salt and pepper, and pour the contents of the pan over the salad. Toss, and serve.

Preparation time

10 minutes

Cooking time

5 minutes

Serves 4

WARM MUSHROOM AND RADICCHIO SALAD WITH PARMESAN

INGREDIENTS

12 medium-sized field mushrooms
3 tbs olive oil
salt and pepper
2 cloves garlic, chopped
1 head of radicchio, cleaned
4 tomatoes, sliced
piece of Parmesan cheese, weighing approx. 125 g/4 oz
fresh parsley, chopped

Heat the grill. Wipe the mushrooms clean, and grill them for 1 minute or so on either side. Meanwhile heat the oil. Transfer the grilled mushrooms to the frying pan, season with salt and pepper, add the garlic, and sauté quickly. Arrange the radicchio leaves and tomato slices on 4 plates. Add 3 grilled mushrooms to each plate. Divide the hot, garlicky olive oil between the plates, and flake the Parmesan cheese on top. Garnish with chopped parsley.

Preparation time

10 minutes

Cooking time

5 minutes

Serves 4

WARM POTATO, ONION, AND RED PEPPER SALAD

Preparation time

5 minutes

Cooking time

15 minutes

Serves 4

Scrub the new potatoes, and put them on to boil in plenty of water for about 10 minutes. Heat 3 tablespoonfuls of oil, and fry the strips of pepper in it. When the potatoes are cooked, drain them, and put them, together with the onion, in a bowl. Add another tablespoonful of oil to the peppers in the pan, and pour them over the potatoes. Toss, season with salt and pepper, and garnish with the chopped herbs.

INGREDIENTS

500 g/1 lb very small new potatoes

4 tbs olive oil

1 red pepper, deseeded, deribbed, and sliced into strips

1 small onion, very finely chopped

salt and a little freshly ground black pepper

1 tbs chopped fresh chives or fresh parsley, or both

GREEK SALAD

Preparation time

10 minutes

Serves 4

Wash and quarter the tomatoes, and put them in a salad bowl with the onion, green pepper, and the cucumber. Add the black olives and the feta cheese. Pour over the olive oil, season with salt and pepper, and sprinkle with the oregano.

INGREDIENTS

250 g/8 oz tomatoes

1 small onion, thinly sliced across, and divided into rings

1 green pepper, deribbed, deseeded, and sliced into strips

1 cucumber, peeled, and sliced paper thin

a handful of black olives

125 g/4 oz Greek feta cheese, cut into cubes

4 tbs olive oil

salt and a little freshly ground black pepper

a pinch of dried oregano

SPICED BULGUR SALAD

INGREDIENTS

125 g/4 oz bulgur
4 or 5 spring onions, finely chopped
3 tomatoes, chopped
a small sprig of fresh mint, chopped
1 tbs chopped fresh parsley
1 tbs chopped fresh coriander
1 cucumber, peeled and chopped
For the dressing:
2 tbs olive oil
1 tbs lemon juice
1 clove garlic, crushed
1 tsp ground cumin
a pinch of chilli powder
salt and pepper

Rinse the bulgur, put it in a bowl, and cover it with cold water. Let it soak for 20 minutes, then drain thoroughly, and squeeze out any excess water. Combine the spring onions, tomatoes, mint, parsley, coriander, and cucumber in a salad bowl. Add the bulgur, and toss together.

To make the dressing, blend the oil, lemon juice, garlic, cumin, chilli powder, and salt and pepper. Pour the dressing over the salad, and toss. Serve chilled.

Preparation time

30 minutes

Serves 4

TUNA AND BEANS

INGREDIENTS

1 large can of tuna in oil
1 large can of cannellini beans
1 small onion, sliced into rings
3 or 4 tinned anchovies
3 or 4 tbs olive oil
salt and pepper
1 tbs chopped fresh parsley

This popular Italian appetizer is a gift for the Superfast Food kitchen, since most of the ingredients can be kept in your store cupboard, and put together in no time.

Drain the tuna, and put it in a salad bowl. Drain the cannellini beans, and add them to the tuna. Add the onion rings. Rinse the anchovies under the cold tap, and blot dry. Chop them, and add them to the salad. Pour over the oil. Season lightly with salt and pepper, and sprinkle with the parsley.

Preparation time

10 minutes

Serves 4

RED BEAN, DAMSON, AND CORIANDER SALAD

Preparation time

5 minutes

Cooking time

10 minutes

Serves 4

A Russian speciality, this salad has an unforgettable taste. It looks good served in a plain, white, china salad bowl. The quantities given make enough for four side-dish servings.

Drain and rinse the beans, and put them in a salad bowl. Peel the garlic, and pound it with the salt. Put it in a small pan together with the vinegar and the damson jam, and, over a low heat, bring the pan very slowly to simmering point. Meanwhile, clean and blot dry the coriander, and chop it very finely – use a food processor, if you have one. When the sauce has liquefied – still without boiling – stir in the coriander, and quickly pour over the beans. Stir very gently with a wooden spoon – a metal one could break up the beans – and leave it to cool.

INGREDIENTS

400 g/14 oz can of red kidney beans
1 clove garlic
a little salt
1 tsp red or white wine vinegar
2½ tbs stoneless damson jam
a bunch of good fresh coriander

THREE-BEAN SALAD

Preparation time

10 minutes

Serves 4

Tip the beans into a sieve, rinse thoroughly in cold water, and blot them dry with kitchen paper. Put the beans in a salad bowl, and garnish with the onion rings and parsley. Mix together the olive oil, vinegar, and salt and pepper, and pour the dressing over the beans. Toss very gently.

INGREDIENTS

400 g/14 oz can of cannellini beans
400 g/14 oz can of red kidney beans
400 g/14 oz can of flageolet beans
1 medium onion, sliced into rings
1 heaped tbs chopped fresh parsley
For the dressing:
3 tbs olive oil
2 tsp balsamic vinegar
salt and freshly ground black pepper

FRENCH DRESSING

INGREDIENTS

1 tsp sea salt

plenty of freshly ground black pepper

1 tsp dried *herbes de Provence*

1 tsp Dijon mustard

450 ml/¾ pt extra-virgin olive oil

100 ml/3 fl oz white wine vinegar

This vinaigrette will keep for up to a month in a clean, stoppered bottle, so that you can have an instant salad dressing whenever you need it – just add garlic to taste when you use the dressing.

Mix the salt, pepper, *herbes de Provence*, and mustard with a little of the oil, and stir to a paste. Add a few drops of wine vinegar, then add the rest of the oil and vinegar, a little at a time.

Preparation time

5 minutes

SAUCES

QUICK TOMATO AND OLIVE SAUCE

Preparation time

2 minutes

Cooking time

15 minutes

Serves 2

This unusual tomato sauce goes beautifully with pasta, or you can serve it with grilled fish or chicken. Black olive tapenade and sun-dried tomatoes can be bought from most large supermarkets. They impart a rich texture and flavour to an otherwise simple sauce.

Heat the oil, fry the onion until it is gilded, then add the tomatoes. Stir, and heat through for a few minutes. Stir in the *tapenade* and the sun-dried tomatoes, heat for a minute or 2, and season to taste with pepper.

INGREDIENTS
2 tbs olive oil
1 onion, chopped
400 g/14 oz can of tomatoes, chopped
3 tbs black olive *tapenade*
2 tbs sun-dried tomatoes, cut into strips
freshly ground black pepper

TOMATO AND LEMON SALSA

Preparation time

5 minutes

Serves 4

This wonderful fresh sauce with a sharp chilli tang is good with grilled fish or chicken, rice, or pasta.

Mix all the ingredients together in a bowl, cover with clingfilm, and chill for at least one hour. You can store the salsa in the refrigerator for 2 or 3 days.

INGREDIENTS
500 g/1 lb ripe red tomatoes, skinned and chopped
2 or 3 cloves garlic, finely chopped
2 tbs chopped fresh coriander, basil, or parsley
8 tbs extra-virgin olive oil
2 tbs fresh lemon juice
4 or 5 spring onions, finely chopped
fresh red or green chilli, to taste, deseeded and chopped

SPICY TOMATO AND ONION SAUCE

INGREDIENTS

50 g/2 oz butter
1 onion, finely chopped
2 cloves garlic, crushed
2 tbs vinegar
150 ml/¼ pt water
1 tbs English mustard
2 tbs demerara sugar
a thick slice of lemon
a pinch of cayenne pepper
2 tbs Worcestershire sauce
6 tbs tomato ketchup
2 tbs tomato purée
salt and freshly ground black pepper

Serve this sauce with pasta, or grilled chicken or fish. You can make a large amount, divide it into smaller quantities, and keep it in the freezer.

Melt the butter in a pan, and sauté the onion and garlic gently for 2 or 3 minutes. Stir in the vinegar, water, mustard, sugar, lemon, and cayenne. Bring to the boil, cover, and simmer for 15 minutes. Stir in the remaining ingredients, season to taste with salt and pepper, and cook for a further 5 minutes. Remove the lemon before serving.

Preparation time

10 minutes

Cooking time

25 minutes

Serves 6-8

SAUCE MORNAY

INGREDIENTS

2 tbs butter
2 tbs flour
300 ml/½ pt milk, heated
a little salt and white pepper
50 g/2 oz hard, strongly flavoured cheese, such as Cheddar, grated
a pinch of crushed dried chilli
a good pinch of nutmeg

This simple, quick sauce is the basis for delicious gratin dishes. Vegetables lend themselves particularly well to the Sauce Mornay treatment – courgettes, cauliflower, broccoli, and young turnips, can be cooked al dente, transferred to an ovenproof dish, covered in Sauce Mornay, and topped with a little grated cheese. Five minutes in a hot oven will produce a delicious dish with a golden-brown topping.

Melt the butter in a saucepan. Stir in the flour, and add the hot milk a little at a time, stirring to keep the sauce smooth. Season with salt and pepper, add the cheese, chilli, and nutmeg, and cook over the lowest possible heat for 5 minutes.

Preparation time

2 minutes

Cooking time

10 minutes

Serves 4

QUICK GARLIC MAYONNAISE

If you have a blender or food processor, you can make this wonderful, thick, yellowy sauce, with the smell and taste of Provence, in just minutes. Eat it with plain grilled or poached fish, with prawns, or with hard-boiled eggs.

Preparation time

5 minutes

Serves 4

If the eggs have been in the refrigerator, warm them a little in a basin of hot water before you crack them. Put the egg yolks, garlic, and salt in the blender or food processor, and blend fast until the yolks are frothy. Then, continuing to blend, begin adding the oil very slowly. Once the mixture has thickened, you can add the rest of the oil quite quickly. Add the lemon juice a little at a time.

If the mayonnaise curdles and thins, pour it into a jug. Put another egg yolk into the blender, blend it briefly, then start adding the contents of the jug, very slowly.

If you prefer a thin mayonnaise, use half extra-virgin olive oil and half a lighter oil, such as sunflower. You can thin the sauce by stirring in a teaspoonful or so of boiling water once it is made.

INGREDIENTS
2 egg yolks
2 fat cloves of garlic, peeled and crushed
a pinch of salt
300 ml/½ pt extra-virgin olive oil
1 tbs freshly squeezed lemon juice

ROUILLE

This is a short-cut version of the famous fiery sauce that the French serve with fish soups. Make it as hot as you like – you can use cayenne instead of chillies, but it should be fresh and strong.

Preparation time

5 minutes

Serves 4

Add the garlic to the mayonnaise, stir in the tomato purée, and add as much chilli as tastes will stand. Traditionally fish soup is served with rouille, grated Swiss cheese, and slices of bread. Each diner takes 3 or 4 slices of bread, slathers rouille on top, dunks them in a plateful of fish soup, and sprinkles over grated cheese. Add trimmings like this to a good bought fish soup, and you can turn it into a feast.

INGREDIENTS
3 or 4 cloves garlic, peeled and crushed
300 ml/½ pt good-quality mayonnaise
5 cm/2 in condensed tomato purée from a tube
crushed dried red chillies, to taste

SNACKS

MICHAEL'S WELSH RAREBIT

INGREDIENTS

175 g/6 oz cheese – red Leicester or mature Cheddar

freshly ground black pepper

2 tbs milk

a little Worcestershire sauce

a pinch of mustard powder

a pinch of paprika

2 thick slices wholewheat bread

To turn this into a more substantial snack, make Buck Rarebit, served with a poached egg on top of each helping. Another variation is Apple Rarebit Savoury. Grill 2 rashers of bacon. Peel a large apple, cut it into 8 slices, and sauté for 2 minutes in a little butter. Serve the bacon and apple with the rarebit.

Heat the grill, and line the grill pan with foil. Grate the cheese into a bowl, add plenty of pepper, and the milk. Mash it with a fork – it should be the consistency of porridge. Add the Worcestershire sauce, mustard powder, and paprika. Toast the bread on one side, then turn it over and divide the mixture between the two pieces. Allow a little gap around the edges, since the mixture will spread. Grill until the topping bubbles and turns brown.

Preparation time

5 minutes

Cooking time

10 minutes

Serves 2

SCRAMBLED EGGS

INGREDIENTS

2 eggs

1 tbs milk

salt and freshly ground black pepper

a big knob of butter

To serve:

wholewheat toast, buttered

Scrambled eggs are one of the great fast-food snacks, and piled invitingly on a piece of buttered wholewheat toast, they're a quick and satisfying meal. Here is the basic version, and two variations.

Beat the eggs with the milk, and season to taste with salt and pepper. Melt the butter in a small non-stick pan. Once it is foaming, remove from the heat, dash in the eggs and start stirring quickly. If you like the eggs a little runny, a couple of minutes will do. If you prefer them cooked firm, return the pan to the heat, and stir until the eggs are sufficiently cooked. Meanwhile, toast the bread, butter it, and serve the eggs on top.

Preparation time

3 minutes

Cooking time

3–5 minutes

Serves 1

SCRAMBLED EGGS LATIN-STYLE

Preparation time

5 minutes

Cooking time

10 minutes

Serves 1

Heat the oil in a small non-stick pan. Fry the onion until soft, add the chopped tomato, the chilli, season to taste with salt and pepper, and fry over a fairly low heat for another 5 minutes. Beat the eggs, add them to the pan, and stir gently for a couple of minutes until they have set to your taste. If you find this dish too hot, substitute a little chilli powder for the whole chilli

INGREDIENTS

1 tbs olive oil

1 small onion, chopped

1 big ripe tomato, chopped

1 small chilli, deseeded and chopped

salt and freshly ground black pepper

2 eggs

SCRAMBLED EGGS WITH SMOKED MACKEREL

Preparation time

12 minutes

Cooking time

5 minutes

Serves 2

Put the mackerel in a basin with the cream, lemon juice, and spring onions, and put aside for 10 minutes. Beat the eggs with a little salt and pepper. Heat the butter in a non-stick saucepan, pour in the eggs, and stir with a wooden spoon. When the eggs are beginning to set, pour in the mackerel mixture, and stir until the eggs have nearly set. Serve on hot plates with buttered wholewheat toast.

INGREDIENTS

125 g/4 oz smoked mackerel, flaked

2 tbs single cream

1 tsp fresh lemon juice

2 or 3 spring onions, cleaned and finely chopped

3 eggs

salt and pepper

1 tbs butter

To garnish:

fresh dill

To serve:

wholewheat toast, buttered

POTATO PANCAKES

INGREDIENTS

500 g/1 lb potatoes
1 medium onion
2 eggs
2 tbs plain flour
salt and pepper
3 or 4 tbs sunflower oil

Peel the potatoes and onion, and grate them into a large bowl. Beat the eggs, and add them, stir in the flour and the salt and pepper. Mix together well. Heat the oil in a frying pan, and fry tablespoonfuls of the mixture, flattening them down in the pan, for 5 minutes on each side.

Preparation time

10 minutes

Cooking time

10 minutes

Serves 4

MUSHROOMS ON TOAST

INGREDIENTS

4 large field mushroom or 250 g/8 oz cultivated mushrooms
3 or 4 spring onions
1 tbs sesame seed oil
2 cloves garlic, finely chopped
salt and pepper
To serve:
4 thick slices wholewheat toast

Clean the mushrooms, cut off the stalks, and chop them. Cut the mushroom caps into big chunks. Trim the spring onions and chop them – include the green stems. Heat the oil in a wok. Add the mushrooms, spring onions, and garlic. Season to taste with salt and pepper. Fry in the hot oil for about 5 minutes, or until the mushrooms are just changing colour, and serve on the hot toast.

Preparation time

5 minutes

Cooking time

5 minutes

Serves 2

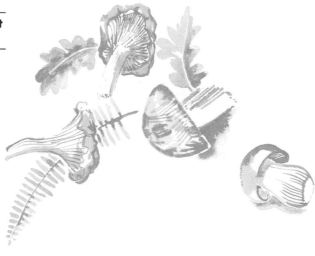

HENRI'S PITA PIZZA

Preparation time

2 minutes

Cooking time

3 minutes

Serves 1

Made with wholewheat pita bread, this is a Superfast, healthy variation on pizza. Try any of the classic pizza toppings, such as anchovies, black olives, thinly sliced onion, slivers of red or green pepper, thin slices of mushroom, diced ham, or slices of pepperoni.

Heat the grill to red hot. Toast the pita on one side for a minute or two, and remove from the grill. Turn the bread over, and top with sliced tomatoes, salt and pepper to taste, oregano, and the grated cheese. Dribble the oil over the top, and return to the grill. The pizzas will be done in 2 to 3 minutes.

INGREDIENTS

1 wholewheat pita

1 medium tomato, sliced

salt and freshly ground black pepper

a good pinch of dried oregano

1 tbs grated Cheddar cheese

1 tsp olive oil

GARLIC BREAD

Preparation time

5 minutes

Cooking time

10–15 minutes

Serves 4

This classic is a useful snack for when the children are suddenly ravenous, and supper time is still hours away.

Heat the oven to 200°C/400°F/gas 6. Mash together the butter, garlic and *fines herbes*. Make vertical cuts all the way along the baguette, not quite through to the bottom. Spread the garlic butter on each slice. Press the bread together, wrap it in foil, and put it in the oven for 10–15 minutes.

INGREDIENTS

50 g/2 oz butter

3 or 4 cloves garlic, crushed

a sprinkling of dried *fines herbes*

a wholewheat or white baguette

HUMMUS

INGREDIENTS

400 g/14 oz can of chickpeas
juice of 1 lemon
1 tsp ground cumin
3 or 4 tbs water
2 cloves garlic, crushed
2 or 3 tbs tahini
a little extra-virgin olive oil
2 tsp paprika

Serve this delicious snack with hot pita bread, black olives, spring onions, and a glass of red wine. The quantities make enough for four people as a main dish, or eight as a snack or starter. You can buy tahini in health food shops.

Drain and thoroughly rinse the chickpeas. Put them in a food processor with the lemon juice, cumin, garlic, and water – start with a couple of tablespoonfuls, and add more if necessary. Process to a rough, creamy paste. Add more water, more lemon juice, more garlic, and more cumin to taste, and some olive oil, if you wish – experiment to find the flavour and texture that appeals to you. When it is ready to serve, place the hummus in a dish, sprinkle the paprika on top, and dribble some olive oil over it. It will keep in the refrigerator for 2 or 3 days, covered with clingfilm.

Preparation time

5–10 minutes

Serves 4-6

GUACAMOLE

INGREDIENTS

2 ripe avocados
juice of 1 lemon
2 cloves garlic, crushed
2 spring onions, finely chopped
1 large beef tomato, skinned and roughly chopped
freshly ground black pepper
fresh coriander, chopped
To serve:
taco chips, hot wholewheat pita bread, or *crudités*

Cut the avocados in half, remove the stones, and liquidize the flesh together with the lemon juice in a blender or food processor. Add all the other ingredients, and blend for a second or two. Serve as soon as possible. If you're not going to eat the guacamole immediately, cover it with clingfilm, and keep it in the refrigerator. If you don't possess a food processor or blender, mash the avocados with a fork, which is easy if they are ripe.

Preparation time

10 minutes

Serves 4-6

MUESLI

Preparation time

5 minutes

Serves 1

Prepare this snack 6–8 hours in advance, or leave it in a cool place, covered, overnight, for an extra-nourishing breakfast that will be almost ready for you in the morning.

Put the oats in a cereal bowl, and add the raisins, and water. Cover, and leave overnight. At breakfast time, wash a small apple, and grate it in. Stir in the lemon juice, and add the cream.

You can also add a spoonful of sesame or sunflour seeds to soak overnight with the oats – by morning they will be soft and chewy.

INGREDIENTS

1 to 2 tbs oat flakes or porridge oats
a few raisins
3 tbs water
1 small apple
2 tsp freshly pressed lemon juice
2 tbs single cream

SANDWICHES

When it comes to sandwich fillings, most people's minds become blank, until they think of cheese. So here are a twelve delicious ideas for sandwiches. Use sliced wholemeal or granary bread, wholemeal baps, baguettes, or an Italian bread, such as ciabatta.

EGG, MAYONNAISE, AND CRESS

Hard-boil the eggs, and shell and mash them with enough mayonnaise to make a creamy filling. Add plenty of cress.

CARROT, CHIVES, AND MAYONNAISE

Clean 1 or 2 carrots, grate them into some mayonnaise, and add a few finely chopped chives.

TOMATO, WATERCRESS, AND MAYONNAISE

Spread some mayonnaise on buttered bread, lay sliced tomatoes on top, season sparingly with salt and pepper, and top with a layer of watercress.

TOMATO, SPRING ONIONS, AND MAYONNAISE

Slice some tomatoes thinly, and clean and slice some spring onions, using plenty of the green parts. Spread mayonnaise on some thinly buttered bread, add the tomatoes, season to taste with salt and pepper, and sprinkle with the spring onions.

TOMATOES, OLIVE OIL, ONION RINGS, BLACK OLIVES, AND BASIL

This is an excellent filling for a big granary roll or bap, or a wholemeal baguette. The longer you leave it, the nicer it will be, since the lovely Mediterranean flavours soak into the bread.

Slice the bread in half, and dribble on plenty of good olive oil – it will soak right into the bread. Top with thinly sliced tomatoes and onion rings, add a few stoned black olives, a few torn fresh basil leaves, season to taste with salt and freshly ground black pepper, and press the other half of the bread well down on top.

CREAM CHEESE, TOASTED SUNFLOWER SEEDS, AND ICEBERG LETTUCE

Toss the sunflower seeds in a pan in a small dribble of olive oil to toast them. Spread some cream cheese on very lightly buttered bread, press the sunflower seeds into it, and cover with a layer of Iceberg lettuce.

CHEDDAR CHEESE, MAYONNAISE, AND SPRING ONIONS

Grate the cheese into just enough mayonnaise to bind it, and mix in a good tablespoonful of chopped spring onions.

SARDINES, LEMON JUICE, AND CHILLI POWDER

Mash a can of sardines with half their weight of soft butter. Add a dash of lemon juice, and a pinch of chilli powder.

TUNA, MAYONNAISE, AND CUCUMBER

Mash a can of tuna with a couple of tablespoons of mayonnaise. Grate in some cucumber, and season well with salt and pepper.

SALMON, FROMAGE FRAIS, DILL, AND SPRING ONIONS

Remove the bones and bits of skin from a tin of salmon, and mash with a spoonful or two of *fromage frais*. Mix in some chopped fresh dill, and 2 or 3 spring onions, finely chopped.

THE PERFECT CUCUMBER SANDWICH

Peel the cucumber, slice it paper-thin, and leave it to drain in a colander for 5 minutes with a little salt. Blot the cucumber dry, and pile it onto very thinly sliced, buttered wholewheat bread. Add a little salt, a drop or two of olive oil, and a little cress, before topping with the other slice of bread.

THE PERFECT TOMATO SANDWICH

Skin the tomatoes, chop them very finely, add some salt and freshly ground black pepper, and some finely chopped chives. Sandwich the tomatoes between thin slices of buttered wholewheat bread.

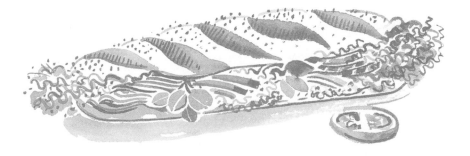

PUDDINGS

For the cook in a hurry, the simplest pudding is a piece of fresh fruit. There are times, however, when either the occasion or the company calls for a little more, but preparing a pudding needn't take longer than a few minutes – the very simplest dishes are usually the most successful.

In summer, when there's a glut of soft fruit, purée them, and serve them as a sauce for ice cream, or whip them up into a fool with Greek yogurt, *fromage frais, crème fraîche*, or real cream if you're feeling luxurious. When peaches, apricots, nectarines, plums, and greengages become plentiful, you can make a simple pudding by stewing them in very little water, fruit juice, wine, or even cheap brandy for just a few minutes. Add a touch of warm spices, such as cardamom, cinnamon, nutmeg, cloves, or allspice, and either eat them hot, or chill them, and serve with cream, yogurt, or *crème fraîche*.

PEACH AND APRICOT COMPOTE

Preparation time

5 minutes

Cooking time

15 minutes

Serves 4

This is a pudding for the summer, when fresh ripe apricots and tiny peaches are cheap and plentiful on every market stall.

Wash the fruit carefully, and put it in a pan with the wine or apple juice, the cinammon stick, and the honey. Bring to the boil, turn the heat right down, and simmer, covered, for about 10–15 minutes, or until the fruit is soft. Chill. Serve with yogurt, *crème fraîche*, or ice cream.

INGREDIENTS
500 g/1 lb small peaches
500 g/1 lb ripe apricots
150 ml/¼ pt white wine or apple juice
a cinnamon stick
1 level tbs honey

WINTER COMPOTE

INGREDIENTS

250 g/8 oz stoned prunes

250 g/8 oz dried apricots

250 g/8 oz dried pears

250 g/8 oz dried apples

125 g/4 oz each seedless raisins and sultanas

125 g/4 oz chopped or flaked almonds

half a lemon, sliced thinly

1 tsp cinnamon

a little ground nutmeg

1 sherry glass of brandy

juice of half a lemon

2 tbs soft brown sugar

This is a traditional, Jewish, winter dessert, that is equally good cold for breakfast.

Preheat the oven to 175°C/350°F/gas 4. In a large casserole dish arrange the dried fruit and lemon slices in layers, with the raisins, sultanas, and almonds sprinkled in between. Sprinkle the cinnamon and nutmeg on top. Mix the brandy, lemon juice, and sugar, and pour over the fruit. Add enough boiling water to cover. Bake in the oven for 20 minutes.

Preparation time

10 minutes

Cooking time

20 minutes

Serves 4

TOFFEE BANANAS

INGREDIENTS

4 bananas

2 tbs brown sugar

4 tbs dark rum

A quick, gooey dessert that goes well with thick yogurt or crème fraîche.

Heat the grill to red hot. Peel the bananas and lay them in a shallow ovenproof dish. Sprinkle them thickly with the brown sugar, and pour the rum around them. Place under the grill until the sugar and rum bubble. Serve immediately.

Preparation time

2 minutes

Cooking time

4 minutes

Serves 4

MONT BLANC

Preparation time

5 minutes

Serves 4

Put the chestnut purée, sugar, orange juice, and rind in a food processor, and blend until smooth. Add 4 tablespoonfuls of the cream or *crème fraîche*, and blend again. Serve heaped in a mound on a pretty dish, topped with the rest of the cream or *crème fraîche*, and sprinkle the grated chocolate on top.

INGREDIENTS
500 g/1 lb can unsweetened chestnut purée
1 tbs brown sugar
rind and juice of 1 orange
6 tbs thick cream or *crème fraîche*
To garnish:
1 tbs grated bitter chocolate

RED PLUM PUDDING

Preparation time

5 minutes

Cooking time

10 minutes

Serves 4

Wash the plums, and put them in a pan with the honey, the wine, and the cardamom pods. Simmer over a low heat until the plums are just starting to disintegrate, then add the brandy (alcohol, incidentally, evaporates when heated, leaving only the flavour behind). Heat through again, and transfer to a serving dish. Serve with cream, yogurt, *fromage frais* or *crème fraîche*. This pudding is also delicious cold.

INGREDIENTS
500 g/1 lb dark red plums
2 tsp runny honey
2 tbs red wine
4–6 cardamom pods
1 tbs cassis or brandy

BAKED APPLES

INGREDIENTS

4 large cooking apples
2 tbs ground almonds
1 tbs orange juice
1 tbs raisins, washed
8 cloves
1 tbs butter
1 tbs brown sugar
a little freshly ground nutmeg

If you are already using the oven, Baked Apples are the perfect choice. They take little more than 20 minutes in a hot oven, or half an hour in a moderate oven. They're delicious served cold, too.

Carefully wash and core the apples. Butter an ovenproof dish, and stand the apples in it – you may have to slice off their bottoms to keep them upright. Stuff the ground almonds and raisins into the cavities, moisten with the orange juice, and stick a couple of cloves in each apple. Then smear a little butter around the top of each apple, and sprinkle with a little sugar. Grind some fresh nutmeg over the tops, and bake until the skins are shiny and just ready to burst.

Preparation time

5 minutes

Cooking time

20–30 minutes

Serves 4

FRUIT CRUMBLE

INGREDIENTS

500 g/1 lb fruit
2 tsp soft brown sugar
2 tbs water
125 g/4 oz oatflakes
125 g/4 oz ground almonds
1 tbs runny honey
2 tbs flaked almonds
50 g/2 oz butter, cut into tiny pieces

You can use many different kinds of fruit for this quick and easy, but very nourishing crumble – apples, plums, rhubarb, blackberries, apricots, or peaches will all do. There's no need to cook the fruit beforehand.

Heat the oven to 200°C/400°F/gas 6. Lightly grease a pie dish. Put in the fruit, washed, and peeled or cut up, if necessary. Add the sugar and the water. Mix together the oats and ground almonds, and spread on top of the fruit – there should be enough to form a coating 2.5 cm/1 inch thick. Drizzle the honey on top, and scatter over the flaked almonds. Dot with the butter, and put in the oven for 20 minutes.

Preparation time

5 minutes

Cooking time

20 minutes

Serves 4

BANANA AND MANGO CRUMBLE

Preparation time

5 minutes

Cooking time

20 minutes

Serves 4

Preheat the oven to 190°C/375°F/gas 5. Mix the mango and banana with the lemon rind, lemon juice, and half the sugar, and pour into a lightly greased pie dish. Knead together the breadcrumbs and the butter, add the remaining sugar and the muesli, and distribute evenly on top of the fruit. Dot with a little more butter. Cook for 20 minutes. Serve with a little single cream.

INGREDIENTS

1 large mango, cubed

4 bananas, peeled and cut in thick slices

grated rind and juice of an unwaxed lemon

2 tbs soft brown sugar

175 g/6 oz wholewheat breadcrumbs

75 g/3 oz butter

2 tbs sugar-free muesli

ORANGE MANGO FOOL

Preparation time

5 minutes

Serves 4

Peel the mangoes, remove the flesh, and put it in a blender or food processor. Add the yogurt and orange juice, and process until smooth. Chill. Decorate with the grated orange rind, and serve.

INGREDIENTS

2 ripe mangoes

150 ml/¼ pt Greek yogurt

grated rind and juice of half an orange

DRINKS

When you're short of time, drinks made in the blender, food processor, or juicer are a quick way to load in the goodness and vitality of fresh fruit and vegetables. Sip these drinks slowly to aid the digestion of the sugars.

COLD BORSCHT

INGREDIENTS

1 medium-sized cooked beetroot, peeled and sliced

4 or 5 sprigs of parsley

150 ml/¼ pt plain yogurt

1 tsp lemon juice

This is a good pick-me-up for times when you're feeling tired and run-down.

Put all the ingredients in the blender, and liquidize.

Preparation time

3 minutes

Serves 1

BANANA BRACER

INGREDIENTS

1 banana, peeled

200 ml/7 fl oz milk

1 tbs plain yogurt

1 tsp honey

2 tsp brewer's yeast

This is a protein-rich drink that makes a good substitute for breakfast when you're too busy to cook.

Put all the ingredients in the blender, and liquidize.

Preparation time

3 minutes

Serves 1

BANANA COOLER

INGREDIENTS

1 banana, peeled

125 ml/4 fl oz unsweetened orange juice

2 or 3 segments of pink grapefruit

3 tbs plain yogurt

A fresh but filling breakfast in a glass.

Put all the ingredients in a blender or food processor, and liquidize.

Preparation time

3 minutes

Serves 1

SUMMER SPECIAL

Preparation time

3 minutes

Serves 1

You could also make this drink in winter, using frozen summer fruit. If you use frozen fruit, put it in a pan, and warm through over a low heat for 2 to 3 minutes.

Put all the ingredients in a blender or food processor, and liquidize.

INGREDIENTS

1 tbs raspberries, washed

1 tbs blackcurrants, washed

150 ml/¼ pt plain yogurt

1 tbs *crème fraîche*

TOMATO REVIVER

Preparation time

3 minutes

Serves 1

Put all the ingredients in a blender or food processor, and liquidize.

INGREDIENTS

2 or 3 fresh, ripe tomatoes, skinned

150 ml/¼ pt plain low-fat yogurt

2 tsp lemon juice

2 or 3 sprigs of parsley

CARROT AND CUCUMBER JUICE

Preparation time

3 minutes

Serves 1

A wonderful cleanser for the whole system.

Process all the ingredients in a juicer.

INGREDIENTS

2 or 3 carrots, carefully scrubbed

a few lettuce leaves

half a small cucumber, well scrubbed

CARROT AND APPLE JUICE

INGREDIENTS

3 or 4 carrots, scrubbed

2 or 3 crisp apples, scrubbed and cored

Make this wonderful drink to boost your resistance. Sip it slowly in the morning.

Process all the ingredients in a juicer.

Preparation time

3 minutes

Serves 1

WINTER GREEN

INGREDIENTS

4 carrots, scrubbed

4 stalks of celery, cleaned

6 spinach leaves

2 or 3 sprigs of parsley

A juicer drink to give your vitality a boost during the grey days of winter.

Process all the ingredients in a juicer.

Preparation time

3 minutes

Serves 1

TUTTI FRUTTI

INGREDIENTS

1 large peach, skinned and stoned

3 or 4 ripe apricots, washed and stoned

1 nectarine, washed and stoned

3 tbs plain yogurt

2 or 3 ice cubes

A liquid fruit salad, this is an ideal drink for summer, when soft fruits are ripe and cheap.

Put all the ingredients in a blender or food processor, and liquidize.

Preparation time

3 minutes

Serves 1

BLACKBERRY AND APPLE JUICE

Preparation time

3 minutes

Serves 1

Put all the ingredients in a blender or food processor, and liquidize.

INGREDIENTS

2 tbs blackberries, washed

150 ml/¼ pt apple juice

1 tbs honey

a pinch of cinnamon

ORANGE SUNRISE

Preparation time

3 minutes

Serves 1

This is a glorious, healthy drink, and a rich source of antioxidant vitamins.

Put all the ingredients in a blender or food processor, and liquidize.

INGREDIENTS

the flesh of a ripe mango, peeled

2 tbs plain yogurt

2 ripe apricots, washed and stoned

2 tbs unsweetened orange juice

THE MENUS

EIGHT MENUS FOR ENTERTAINING

SPRING

1

Watercress Soup (p.79) with
wholewheat rolls.
Braised Chicken (p.110).
New potatoes.
Rocket and fennel salad with Brie.
Pears poached in wine with cream.

2

Watercress, Avocado, and Bacon
Salad (p.138).
Chicken in Chablis (p.112).
Turnip and Potato Cream (p.127).
Spinach Italian-Style (p.129).
Selection of cheese with celery and
fresh fruit.

SUMMER

1

Melon with a little chopped
preserved ginger.
Pepper-Crusted Fish in a Warm Lime
and Coriander Vinaigrette (p.93).
New potatoes.
Steamed baby courgettes.
Strawberries and raspberries with
crème fraîche.

2

Cold Cucumber and Yogurt
Soup (p.83).
Fish Baked in a Parcel (p.94).
Quick Garlic Mayonnaise (p.146).
New potatoes tossed in butter
and mint.
Watercress salad.
Peach and Apricot Compote (p.156).

AUTUMN

1

Fresh Tomato Soup (p.81).
Daube of Beef with Tomato
and Olives (p.113).
Baked potatoes.
Spinach puréed with a little cream.
Fruit Crumble (p.159) with Greek
yogurt or *crème fraîche*.

2

Hummus (p.151) with pita bread
and black olives.
Lamb and Pine Kernel Koftas (p.102).
Spiced rice.
Sharp green salad with mint
and rocket.
Selection of cheese with grapes.

WINTER

1

Stilton Soup (p.82).
Duck Breasts with Orange
Juice (p.107).
Broccoli tossed in olive oil
and lemon.
Dried apricots simmered in orange
and Cointreau, with *crème fraîche*.

2

Potted Prawns (p.92) with whole-
wheat toast and lemon wedges.
Lamb Peperonata (p.103).
Baked potatoes.
Watercress salad.
Stilton cheese with walnuts
and tangerines.

LAST-MINUTE MENUS

*Here are eight delicious, yet simple, menus that you can put together quickly
after a last-minute dash around the supermarket for the ingredients.*

SPRING

1

White Bean Soup with Garlic and
Parsley (p.81).
Hot wholewheat rolls.
Mixed green salad.
Stewed apples with *fromage frais*.

2

Spaghetti with Pesto and Green
Vegetables (p.122).
Mixed green salad.
Fresh pears.

SUMMER

1

Courgette Omelette Gratin (p.85).
Green salad.
Hot wholewheat rolls.
Brie.
Fresh peaches and nectarines.

2

Red and Yellow Eggs (p.89).
Braised Fennel (p.129).
Mixed green salad.
Strawberries with Greek yogurt or
crème fraîche.

AUTUMN

1

Ready-made hummus served with
black olives, spring onions, and
hot pita bread.
Henri's Mediterranean Steak (p.100).
Mixed green salad.
Lightly stewed frozen raspberries
with plain yogurt.

2

Fishcakes (p.97).
Cauliflower Gratin II (p.131).
Mixed green salad.
Bunch of grapes.

WINTER

1

Chicken with Garlic (p.104).
Quick Mashed Potatoes (p.127).
Spinach purée.
Chicory and watercress salad.
Cheese and apples.

2

Spaghetti with Meatball and Tomato
Sauce (p.122).
Broccoli with Garlic and
Chilli (p.132).
Chicory and rocket salad.
Stewed apples with lemon and
fromage frais.

A-Z OF SUPERFOODS

*F*oods are incredibly complex. They are all made up of numerous chemical compounds, any one of which may influence our health and wellbeing in a number of different ways. Diligent research has identified a number of these compounds, and established them as vital nutrients, such as vitamins, minerals, amino acids, and fats, but only the surface has been scratched. Scientists today, examining common foods, like apples, carrots, onions, and cabbage, are discovering a host of substances in them which have exciting potential for our health.

In the following list of Superfoods, some of the nutrients known to be found in various foods have been mentioned. We should never forget, however, that these are only part of the story, and that in isolation, such nutrients may have far less value for us biologically than in the whole complex of a fruit, grain, or vegetable.

Sir Robert McCarrison, one of the greatest nutritional experts, said over half a century ago: "It will be found ... that all elements and complexes necessary for normal nutrition ... are present in the fresh fruits of the Earth as nature furnishes them, though not in these foodstuffs as man mishandles and maltreats them."

Almonds are a highly concentrated food, rich in protein (they have a third more protein than eggs), in good fats, B vitamins and vital minerals, like zinc, magnesium, potassium, and iron. Sprinkle almonds on yogurt or stewed fruit, toast them and add them to muesli, or use them in Fruit Crumble topping *(see page 159)*.

Apples One of the great fast foods, apples are the perfect snack. "If you could plant only one tree in your garden, it should be an apple tree", said the French herbalist, Maurice

Messegue. So what's in an apple? They are treasures of natural goodness – the pectin and vitamin C in apples help keep cholesterol levels stable, while pectin also protects us from the ravages of pollution by binding to heavy metals in the body, like lead or mercury, and carrying them safely out. The malic and tartaric acids in apples help neutralize the acid by-products of digestion, and help your body cope with excess protein and rich, fatty foods. Apple purée with pork, apples with cheese, or sage and apple stuffing for goose are shrewd combinations based on traditional country wisdom.

Supermarkets are responding to consumer demand by promoting numbers of traditional apples, some not seen for half a century. Make the most of this choice. Eat apples raw with cheese, a roll, and a green salad for a perfect balanced meal; eat them grated in yogurt and in Muesli *(see page 152)*; stew them lightly, with a cool touch of lemon, in summer, and with warming spices in winter; bake apples stuffed with dried fruit for a simple pudding *(see page 159)*.

Apricots are loaded with beta-carotene, as their yellow-orange colour informs us. Eat them fresh in the summer, when they're cheap and plentiful – choose those that are deeply coloured, soft, and ripe. Dried apricots are a good source of iron in winter, but wash them carefully to remove the sulphur dioxide used as a preservative. Pour boiling water over them, and leave them to soak overnight for a lovely breakfast, or stew and purée them with yogurt or with *fromage frais* for a delicious pudding.

Artichokes, globe are the friend of the liver, as any Frenchman will tell you – an excellent excuse for enjoying this vegetable while it's in season. Artichokes are quick and easy to

prepare. Clean them thoroughly, shake them dry, put them into boiling water, and simmer until you can easily plunge a knife into the thickest part. Serve artichokes with Quick Garlic Mayonnaise *(see page 146)*, or French Dressing *(see page 143)*. Artichoke hearts preserved in olive oil are a useful store cupboard item. Serve them with tomatoes and black olives for a Mediterrean *antipasto*, use them with garlic and a little cream to make a quick pasta sauce, or add them to a bean salad.

Avocado pears are almost a complete food, since they supply oil, mainly in the form of monounsaturated fat, as well as a little protein and starch. The avocado is rich in potassium, deficiency in which can cause fatigue, depression, and poor digestion. It is also a good source of vitamin A, some B-complex vitamins, a little vitamin C, and some vitamin E.

Women in particular, who are often warned off avocados because of their high fat and calorific content should, in fact, eat plenty of this fruit for the sake of their skins. Exciting new research in Israel and California shows that substances in the pulp of avocados appear to trigger DNA to produce more embryonal collagen, which helps keep the skin smooth and supple.

There is no need to fuss with complicated dressings: avocados are delicious eaten with nothing more than a squirt of fresh lemon juice, a little sea salt, and freshly ground black pepper. They also star in some delicious salads, while if you have a blender or food processor, you can whip up Guacamole *(see page 151)* in five minutes, to enjoy with taco chips or hot wholewheat pita bread.

Bananas Another of nature's great fast foods, bananas are high in potassium and antioxidant vitamins, and rich in pectin, a particularly useful form of fibre, which helps the body to eliminate toxic wastes. Reach for a banana instead of the biscuit tin, or blend bananas into a high-energy drink to give you an instant lift when you're feeling low (see page 161).

Beans are one of the mainstays of traditional peasant cookery around the world, and a major source of protein and minerals in the diets of millions of people. Fortunately for the fast-feeder, they're almost as good canned, with the long soaking and cooking already done. Cans of various beans, such as haricot, cannellini, borlotti, black-eyed, and red kidney beans, should feature in your store cupboard, ready to be turned into rich, savoury soups, stews, and salads.

Beans can cause wind, which is why in traditional bean recipes they're invariably cooked with herbs or spices, such as cumin, coriander, caraway, mint, savory, or fennel, that counter this effect.

Beetroot In Romany medicine, beetroot was considered a blood-builder, wonderful for people who were run-down and peaky. Enjoy its smooth, earthy tang, not just cooked, but also grated raw in salads. Try it in a salad with cottage cheese, toasted sunflower seeds, spring onions, plenty of parsley, and a dollop of vinaigrette.

Blackcurrants were once described as "a fruit favouring longevity", and since they're especially rich in vitamin C – vital protection against cancer and heart disease – this reputation seems well-founded. Hot blackcurrant juice is a country remedy for sore throats. One of the most delectable of summer fruits, blackcurrants can be puréed fresh and raw, and stirred into Greek yogurt or *crème fraîche*. They can also be lightly stewed, and eaten hot or cold, or, like bilberries, combined with apples in a crumble (see page 159).

Blueberries are best known as one of the summer fruits, or forest fruits, familiar in the ranks of sweetened, flavoured yogurts. Enjoy this delicious berry fresh and uncooked during its

brief summer season, and for winter, keep a supply of blueberries in the freezer to make into rich, spiced compotes. You can also combine them with apples in a crumble (see page 159), or purée them to make a wickedly good sauce for ice cream.

Bread Say bread anywhere in the Western World, and most people will understand – bread made from wheat. For most of us it is literally our daily bread, often eaten at every single meal of the day. So most of the time it should be wholewheat bread – see the table on page 22, and you'll understand why – in the form of sliced or unsliced loaves, baps, huge soft rolls, or Middle Eastern pita bread, now on sale everywhere. If you shop rarely, keep a supply of rolls, wholewheat pitas, and sliced bread in the freezer. Bread isn't just something, however, that you pile the butter on. In southern Europe it's often fried in oil with garlic and used as a thickening for soups. In Italy a number of rustic salads are made with bread, sun-ripened tomatoes, and olive oil as their chief ingredients – try the recipe for Bread and Tomato Salad, on page 37.

Brewer's yeast A food supplement rather than a Superfood, brewer's yeast is, however, an unrivalled source of the B-complex vitamins, and valuable minerals, including iron, zinc, chromium, magnesium, and potassium. It is also high in protein. Try it in drinks, blended with yogurt, milk, and fruit juice for a massive boost to your depleted nutritional reserves.

Broccoli helps keep cancer at bay, and it is a gourmet food when it is cooked as a fast food – overcooking ruins it. Eat it in a famous sauce for pasta (see page 124), gratinéed – a meal in itself – or simply cooked *al dente*, and spiked with lemon, garlic, or chilli.

Cabbage, like broccoli, is a member of the crucifer family of vegetables, famous for their anti-carcinogenic properties. In population studies, those eating the most cabbage have been

shown to be least likely to develop cancers. Like broccoli, cabbage needs to be cooked only briefly to be at its best, both gastronomically as well as nutritionally. See pages 125–6 for quick ways to prepare it.

Carrots are another of the great Superfoods, so rich in beta-carotene that a carrot or two should supply your vitamin A needs for an entire day – a good reason for eating carrots as often as possible. Carrots are quick and easy to prepare, and can be eaten raw. Grate them into a salad, or dress a dish of grated carrots with a spoonful of vinaigrette and a few almonds and raisins. Carrots are indispensable in a good thick soup – see the recipe for lovely, rich Carrot Soup on page 82.

Celery helps to calm the nerves, according to Hippocrates, perhaps because of its high calcium content. It also has a strong effect on the kidneys, helping to eliminate wastes via the urine. It has a worldwide reputation as an antirheumatic, justified by modern research. Eat celery in season, when it is young and crisp, in the company of a good cheese – it's an even better partner to cheese than bread – or chopped into a crunchy winter salad with apples and walnuts.

Chicken Choose free-range chicken when possible: it costs more than battery chicken, but it is definitely tastier, lower in saturated fats, and free of the many chemicals poured into the battery bird from birth to death. Free-range or not, chicken is in any case much lower in fat than red meat, quicker to cook, and cheaper. You'll find plenty of ideas for cooking this versatile bird in the Recipes (see pages 103–106 and 110–113).

Chickpeas Nutritionally, chickpeas are among the most valuable of the pulses. They are particularly rich in iron, zinc, and magnesium, as well as being an excellent source of fibre and protein. Canned chickpeas can be used to make a rough-and-ready Hummus in minutes (see page 151). Served with a bunch of radishes, a little dish of black olives, and some hot wholewheat pita bread, this makes a delicious, light, summer luncheon.

Chickpeas are good for warming winter soups, too. If you're in a real hurry, fry a sliced onion and some garlic in a pan, add a litre of vegetable stock made from a stock cube, tip in a packet of mixed vegetables, simmer for five minutes, then add a can of chick-peas, rinsed and drained, heat them through, and garnish with some chopped fresh herbs.

Chicory is one of a family of winter salad vegetables – other members are endives and radicchio. All are related to wild chicory, which has always had a powerful reputation in traditional medicine as a cleanser and detoxicant. The touch of bitterness in its flavour recommends it to gourmets, and also indicates that it is good for the liver.

Chicory can be eaten fresh and raw, but it is also excellent cooked, braised in a covered pan for a few minutes, in a tablespoonful of water, with a few rashers of bacon, a couple of cloves of garlic, a touch of lemon juice or vinegar, and a little olive oil or chilli to enhance the flavour. In Italy, they serve radicchio – which is quite tough as a salad leaf – brushed with olive oil, and lightly grilled.

Dates, like figs, are a highly energiz-ing and nourishing foodstuff. Fresh dates are widely available now – much nicer, and certainly less sticky than the boxed kind. Jane Grigson advises splitting them to remove the stone before eating, to check for possible insect eggs. She recommends serving chopped dates with toasted nuts in plain creamy yogurt. Pack dates into the children's school lunch boxes, instead of biscuits. Fresh figs, too, are appearing further and further afield. Exported figs are pricey, however, and dried figs, steamed, or plumped up by soaking in hot water, are better value.

Eggs Another of the great, natural fast foods, eggs are useful little packages of protein, vital minerals, such as iron and zinc, and vitamins. There are dozens of different ways of cooking this versatile food (see pages 84–89), the majority of them as fast as even the most hard-pressed of cooks could wish for.

Fish is an excellent source of protein, wonderfully low in fat compared to meat, and by definition free-range, which means that it is untainted by farmyard chemicals. Sadly, know-ledgable neighbourhood fishmongers are a dying breed, so if you know a good one, it is in your own interests to help keep him in business.

Fish is faster food to prepare than meat. Whether you fry, grill, poach, braise, or bake fish, it's usually done to a turn in minutes, and it lends itself well to cooking in foil or baking-paper parcels, which means there's no smell to linger, and no mess to clear up.

Frozen fish is second-best to fresh, but it can be cooked straight from the freezer, without you having to wait for it to defrost, so a few frozen fish fillets or steaks are always a useful stand-by. In the Recipes (see pages 90–99), you'll find plenty of ideas for cooking both fresh and frozen fish. See also *Oily fish*, overleaf.

Garlic is the king of all healing plants. No other plant has enjoyed such a reputation in so many different countries and civilizations, for helping such a wide range of ailments, and no plant has been the subject of more intensive modern research, confirming the centuries-old reputation that garlic is good for the heart and the lungs, and that it helps keep you young.

Nobody needs a medical reason, however, for eating garlic. Salads, pasta sauces, mayonnaise, casseroles, stews, soups, and several different snacks from around the world – including Guacamole and Hummus (see page 151) – would be lost without it. Eat plenty of garlic to give relish and variety to your daily eating, and to keep you healthy.

Grapes You can eat grapes all year round, thanks to the miracles of modern packaging and transport, although they are at their best in season, when they are irresistibly fresh, ripe, and juicy. Grapes are a real Superfast Food – it would be virtually criminal to cook them, and much the best way to enjoy them is just to eat them as they come. If you eat grapes in midwinter, have them in the form of raisins or sultanas. Great sweet snacks on their own, these can also be soaked overnight to plump them up, and added to muesli, or made into a dried fruit compote (see page 157).

Kiwi fruit This little fruit with the shabby fur coat is a treasury of nutritional riches. It contains almost twice as much vitamin C as oranges, more fibre than apples, and as much vitamin E as avocados.

Kiwi fruits are often bargain-priced in markets: choose those soft enough to yield to gentle pressure. They can be stored in the refrigerator, and should be peeled just before eating. The nicest way to eat them is also the fastest: like a boiled egg, cut off the tops, and scoop out the pale green flesh with its small black seeds.

Lamb is healthier to eat than beef, since it is lower in fat, and free-ranging during its brief life. Lamb with onion or mint sauce are classic combinations, that both aid its digestion. Lamb lends itself naturally to the delicious spicing of Middle Eastern cookery (try the recipe for Lamb Koftas on page 102), for which you can buy lamb ready-minced in most supermarkets. Minced lamb is also useful for making burgers (see page 102) and stir-fries.

Lemons are indispensable to any well-run kitchen, with numerous uses: in salad dressings, to sharpen up flavours, and to give zest to sauces. A squeeze of lemon juice is often the only relish a plain grilled fish needs, and how bland smoked fish would be without it. When strawberries have begun to lose the initial, full flavour of the season, liven them up by cutting the strawberries up and adding to them a tablespoonful of lemon juice and a little sugar.

Lemons are thought of as an acidic fruit. Their sharpness is due to organic acids that are metabolized during digestion to produce potassium carbonate, which actually helps to neutralize acidity.

Milk is practically synonymous in the public mind with calcium, which is why you should drink plenty of milk for your bones' sake. Full-cream milk also contains some vitamin A, D, and E, semi-skimmed milk less, and skimmed milk none. These vitamins, however, are mainly found in the cream, which has had such a bad press over the last few decades – it is high in fat and promotes cholesterol – that many people shudder at the idea of adding a tablespoonful of double cream – 5.7 g/0.2 oz of saturated fat – to a soup or pudding, although they may think nothing of eating their way through a bag of potato crisps – approximately 36 g/1.3 oz of fat. Small amounts of cream can do wonders for dozens of Superfast Food dishes.

If you do worry about the fat content of milk, use *fromage frais* instead, which behaves like cream, but comes in low-fat, very-low-fat, and virtually fat-free forms. Alternatively, try *crème fraîche* – cream that has been lightly fermented after undergoing pasteurization. This is good for cooking and eating with puddings, for its delicious tartness.

For many people, milk can present digestive problems, due to a lack of the enzyme lactase, needed to digest the lactose in milk. Or they may have an allergy or sensitivity to milk. If milk affects you in this way, try one of the new lactose-free milks.

Mushrooms are good, earthy food and can add body and flavour to numerous dishes, or make an excellent snack, simply grilled or fried, and served on a slice of wholewheat toast. Supermarkets stock a wide range of mushrooms, including the exotic *shiitake*, oyster, and chestnut mushrooms. Try a salad of three or four different varieties of mushrooms, dressed with plenty of olive oil, chopped garlic, and parsley. When adding mushrooms to a stew or casserole, put them in only minutes before the end of the cooking time.

Nuts are densely packed with nourishment. Walnuts are the most nutritious of all the nuts. They contain more than 10 per cent protein by weight, as well as zinc, magnesium, iron, potassium, B vitamins, vitamin E, and polyunsaturated fats. Brazil nuts, as well as being rich in protein, also contain vitamin B1 and magnesium, both vital to the nervous system. Hazelnuts have the lowest fat content of all nuts; peanuts are good sources of protein and iron; and pine nuts have the highest protein levels of any nut. Walnuts, chestnuts, and hazelnuts contain Omega-3 fatty acids, which are vital to our health, but are often missing from Western diets. Nuts make a splendid addition to vegetarian dishes, or an agreeable garnish for salads. Use them either plain, or tossed in a non-stick pan to toast them lightly.

Because of their high fat content, nuts go rancid quickly once shelled. Eat them freshly shelled whenever possible, and buy shelled nuts only in small quantities at a time, from shops with a high turnover. Once opened, store them in a screw-top jar, and use them up quickly.

Oats have been the staple diet of some of the hardiest races in history. Not surprisingly, since they are richly nutritious, containing over 12 per cent protein by weight, as well as polyunsaturated fats, a little vitamin E, and plenty of vitamin B. They are also spectacularly high in the minerals and vitamins essential for a healthy nervous system and strong bones and teeth. Eat oats, and you're doing your arteries a real favour – oats supply plenty of silicon for healthy arterial walls, while their role in combating high levels of blood cholesterol and in regulating blood fats is causing great excitement in medical circles today.

Eat oats in the form of porridge or muesli. Use oatmeal instead of flour to dust burgers or fish for frying. Oats also make an excellent topping for fruit crumble *(see page 159).*

Oily fish are an outstanding food. They were once avoided because of their high fat content, but we're now urged to eat them because the fats in oily fish supply high levels of eicosapentanoeic acid, from the Omega-3 family of fatty acids, vital to healthy cell function and brain activity. Salmon, tuna, mackerel, herrings, anchovies, pilchards, and sardines can be quick and easy to prepare, and are readily available canned.

Eat them in salads, mashed up with a little mayonnaise for sandwiches, in fishcakes and fish pies, or smoked – but avoid those with deep yellow or brown dyes. When possible, enjoy fried or grilled anchovies and sardines, freshly hauled out of the sea. In colder climates, fresh herring and mackerel are available, but choose them carefully: they should be firm to the touch and bright-eyed. If they look tired, flabby, and hungover, you're better off eating them from a can. Anchovies add piquancy to a number of pasta sauces. You can save yourself the fiddle and waste of opening a tin or jar, and extracting and chopping just a couple of fillets, by using anchovy paste instead from a tube.

Olive oil Extra-virgin olive oil is king of all the oils, both for its unrivalled flavour, and because it is so good for you. The heart, liver, and digestive system benefit from the goodness of this rich, golden oil, untainted by chemicals. Because extra-virgin olive oil is produced by pressure, rather than by intensive chemical processing, its antioxidants are preserved to give it maximum biological value.

In the Superfast Food kitchen, it is the preferential oil, and well worth the expense. Its special tang is essential to numerous Mediterranean dishes, such as pastas, grills, and salads, that would lose much of their appeal if made with tasteless oils.

Olives, green or black, are a delicious snack, and much healthier than crisps or over-salted nuts. Buy them loose, canned, or in jars. If they're preserved in brine, drain this off, rinse them, and dry them. Keep olives in a screw-top jar – fill it up with olive oil, and add fresh herbs, pieces of fresh red chilli, or chopped garlic. This way the olives will taste delicious, keep for weeks, and you can use up the oil in another dish, such as pasta sauce.

Olive pastes, composed of plain, mashed, black or green olives, are handy for sauces and snacks. Black olive paste is particularly delicious on grilled wholewheat bread. *Tapenade*, a Mediterranean spread, is made with black olives, capers, garlic, and anchovy fillets. This can be found ready-made in many supermarkets, and is delicious for summer lunches, spread on fresh crusty bread.

Onions are one of the three or four absolute basics in any kitchen, and it's hard to imagine soups, stews, and casseroles without them. Fry an onion, and people at once assume that you're cooking something delicious. You're certainly cooking something healthy: onions help keep blood fats stable, and are beneficial eaten with rich foods, like steak, liver, or a cooked breakfast. Eat plenty of onions – especially in winter – and they'll help to keep your respiratory system hale and hearty.

Oranges The high beta-carotene and vitamin C content of oranges – at least when they have been recently picked or juiced – accounts for much of their benign influence on our health. Blood oranges are particularly high in beta-carotene. Eat oranges in winter, when they arrive newly ripe from Spain, Italy, and Morocco.

When you're buying orange juice, make sure that it has no added sugar – analyses in Great Britain of so-called unsweetened orange juices revealed that over half actually contained added sugar. Your taste buds are probably the most reliable guide to this.

Pineapples are rich in vitamins, and particularly good for the digestion, but they need to be eaten absolutely ripe, otherwise they can be sharp and almost sour to the taste. Test for ripeness by pulling a leaf – if it comes gliding out with a gentle tug, the pineapple is ripe, and can be peeled and sliced for a delicious pudding that needs nothing else doing to it. Like

many other fruit, pineapples are now available canned in unsweetened fruit juices instead of syrup. Although they can never be a substitute for fresh pineapple, they do make a welcome addition to fruit salads.

Potatoes must provide a pretty good nutritional package, since they allowed the Irish peasantry to live on almost nothing else for generations, without any obvious health problems. Very much a Superfood, potatoes supply fibre, vitamin B, useful minerals, and just enough vitamin C to keep scurvy at bay. Try to buy organically grown potatoes, free of pesticide residues that are concentrated in the skins, which are nutritionally the vegetable's most valuable part.

Potatoes are not a particularly fast food, although small new potatoes can be boiled in under 15 minutes. For a quickly prepared potato dish, try also Quick Mashed Potatoes *(see page 127)*. Although potatoes can take up to an hour to bake, they need no more than a quick, thorough scrub and a few jabs with a fork by way of preparation.

Pumpkin seeds are an excellent snack food, supplying protein and B vitamins. They can be deep-fried, or tossed in a non-stick pan, and added to salads, or eaten on their own. In many parts of the world – Eastern Europe particularly – they are reputed to be a male sexual tonic and beneficial to the prostate gland.

Raspberries Among the most wonderful of all fruit, raspberries are as health-giving as they are delicious. They are never tastier than when eaten plain and fresh, with perhaps a dollop of *crème fraîche*. They combine beautifully, too, with other berries, such as blackcurrants. Don't store raspberries too long, since they attract mould very quickly. If you find that you can't eat them up within a day, wash them quickly, put them in a pan with a couple of teaspoonfuls of sugar, cover the pan, and put it on the lowest possible heat for just a couple of minutes, or long enough for the juices to begin to run.

Rice, brown The dietary staple of the East is a marvellous food, rich in minerals and B–complex vitamins. When it is polished to whiteness, however, it loses much of its value. White rice is, nonetheless, almost universally preferred. It is lighter than brown rice, it looks more attractive, and it cooks in half the time. There are still possibilities, however, for the Superfast Food cook to use brown rice. You can buy easy-cook or quick-cook brown rice, which takes 20–30 minutes to cook, instead of 45 minutes or more. Ready-cooked brown rice is also available canned. Although it tends to be a bit on the dry side, it is perfectly good stirred into a soup to give it extra body.

On its own, brown rice is much more interesting than white, and if you're pushed for time to do anything more complicated, simply cook it, serve it with a knob of butter and a little grated cheese, and eat it with a salad or a green vegetable. You can make a delicious risotto-style dish with brown rice by preparing the other ingredients while you boil the rice in a separate pan, and combining them once the rice is cooked. Try the quick version of Tomato Risotto with sun-dried tomatoes, on page 118. Brown rice also makes an excellent salad. Stir the oil and other salad ingredients quickly into cooked brown rice while it is still warm, and allow to cool.

Sesame seeds, prized in ancient civilizations for their beneficial effect on sexual health, and for promoting longevity, are rich in nutrients and healthy fats. Like all seeds and nuts, they should be bought fresh, in small quantities, stored in the refrigerator, once opened, and eaten within days. Choose sesame seeds that are dark beige, rather than pale and clean. The darker seeds have probably been mechanically hulled, while the paler ones have had their skins stripped off by bleaching chemicals that may destroy or deform their vital components, as well as leaving undesirable residues. A visual test will tell you: mechanically hulled seeds retain their little black tips.

Add sesame seeds to muesli, toast them and use them in salads, or include them in fruit crumble toppings. They also come pounded into a creamy paste, tahini, an ingredient of *hummus bi tahina* – for a fast version of this dish, see page 151.

Spinach Full of the dark green plant "blood", chlorophyll, spinach is rich in minerals and antioxidants. If you don't have time to prepare it fresh, it comes frozen both in leaves and ready-puréed. Prepare it with a little butter and grated nutmeg.

Sunflower seeds Nutritious and incredibly cheap, sunflower seeds are available freshly hulled in most super-markets. They should be a pale beige-grey colour, with a fine, fresh flavour – if they taste at all rancid, or are starting to turn yellow-brown, discard them.

Sunflower seeds tossed in a non-stick pan for a few moments are a lovely, crunchy addition to salads. You can also add them to home-made Muesli *(see page 152)*. They're an excellent addition to the school lunch box. Smokers trying to quit will find that chewing sunflower seeds can be particularly helpful.

Tomatoes Deep red, sun-ripened tomatoes are one of the great treats of summer, and, at long last, super-markets have begun to stock tomatoes grown for flavour, instead of the watery objects with a chemical taste that we were offered for so long. Make the most of good fresh tomatoes in their season by using them in salads, and in lightly cooked sauces for pasta or rice. The rest of the year, whole, canned tomatoes are a good stand-by. Most of the beta-carotene and vitamin C in tomatoes survives the canning process. Concentrated tomato purée can be a useful addition to soups and stews: buy it in tubes rather than cans.

There are fashions in food just as much as frocks, and sun-dried tomatoes are one of the flavours of the month. Once a deli extravagance, sun-dried tomatoes are now available in jars in many supermarkets. They can add a special authentic flavour to pasta sauces or risottos *(see page 118)*. Keep sun-dried tomatoes topped up with olive oil – you can use it again later – and they will last for ages.

Turnips are a forgotten vegetable for many people, yet their delicious smoky taste can provide a welcome change from potatoes and carrots in winter. Turnips are at their best when they're small and tender, and they may not even need to be peeled. The older, bigger ones can be tough, woody, and taste acrid. Turnips make wonderful soups, and French lamb stews are unthinkable without them. If you don't fancy them on their own, try Turnip and Potato Cream *(see page 127)*.

Watercress is a real health food. It is rich in beta-carotene and vitamin C, while the compounds that impart its peppery bite have been shown in research to have a markedly antibiotic effect. Watercress needs to be washed very carefully, and trimming it can be fiddly, but if you want to save time, some supermarkets supply it ready-washed and trimmed. If you make Watercress Soup *(see page 79)*, you can fling in all but the toughest stalks. Watercress also makes a good addition to sandwiches and salads.

Yogurt is one of dozens of fermented foods eaten and enjoyed around the world. It has a beneficial action in the gut, where it helps promote a healthy intestinal flora. Very-low-fat yogurts are available, but even the rich, creamy Greek yogurts are fairly low in fat, at 10 per cent fat by weight.

Avoid yogurts that are stuffed with synthetic colourings, flavourings, and sugar, as many are, especially those aimed at children. If you want to give children a fruity yogurt, stir in a little fresh or cooked fruit, such as apple or pear purée, unsweetened fruit concen-trate, apricots that have been soaked overnight, summer fruits from the freezer, or a few fresh raspberries or strawberries in season. If you really crave a little sweetness, then add a teaspoonful of honey and some nuts.

HERBS AND SPICES

*W*hen you're pushed for time, meals dished up in a hurry can become repetitive, not to say monotonous. This is where herbs and spices can add savour, piquancy, and zest to your cooking. A windowsill, or corner of the garden, for growing fresh herbs, and a well-stocked spice rack are indispensable to the Superfast kitchen. The herbs and spices used in traditional cookery around the world almost all have a beneficial action on the digestive system, and according to recent research, their essential oils can have an antioxidant effect.

Basil Keep a fresh basil plant on the windowsill in summer, and use the leaves with tomatoes, in pasta sauces, and in summer salads and soups.

Bay One of the ingredients of the classic French *bouquet garni*, bay leaves lend a distinctive flavour to soups, stews, and marinades.

Caraway is an aid to digestion – add a sprinkle of the seeds to bean and cabbage dishes to help reduce their flatulent effect.

Cardamom Use a few of the little green pods when you are preparing a dish of stewed fruit – they will impart a distinctive, warm, spicy flavour.

Chilli Fresh, whole dried, flaked, or in the form of cayenne pepper, a dash of chilli can be a shot in the arm to many dishes. Try a little in warming winter soups, bean dishes, and Latin American *salsas (see page 144).*

Chives have a mild flavour of onions. Use them lavishly in the summer, chopped up in salads and for garnishing cold soups.

Cinnamon Add a stick or two of this distinct but delicate spice when you cook apples, apricots, peaches, and plums for pudding.

Cloves tend to be underused in savoury dishes. Try adding a single clove to beef stew or braised game.

Coriander Rub crushed coriander seeds into the skin of pork or lamb before roasting it. Coriander is used to impart an unmistakable pungent flavour to dishes *(see page 93).*

Cumin is indispensable if you enjoy Mexican, Middle Eastern, or Indian cookery. Toss cumin seeds in a non-stick pan over a low heat to release their aroma.

Dill The feathery fronds are delicious in sauces for fish, or added to sour cream to serve with baked potatoes. Use the seeds with cucumbers and fish, and in sandwiches *(see page 155).*

Fennel is an aid to the digestion, and a good accompaniment to rich fish, like salmon. Add the dark green fronds to mayonnaise to serve with cold fish.

Ginger Fresh ginger root can enhance the flavour of meat and fish, or transform a simple dish of stewed fruit into a party piece.

Horseradish Try a little of the fresh root grated into salad dressing or mayonnaise, or add it to natural yogurt to serve with smoked fish.

Mint Grow a pot of mint to use in salads, tomato sauces, and *tabbouleh*. Use chopped mint lavishly when you make meat balls and burgers to enhance their flavour.

Nutmeg Freshly grated nutmeg adds zest to winter puddings, while green vegetables are much improved by a good sprinkle of this warm spice. Always use whole fresh nutmegs.

Oregano has the aroma that says Italian cookery. Almost as good dried as fresh, oregano is used widely in pizzas and tomato-based sauces.

Parsley deserves to be used lavishly – it contains a wealth of vitamins and minerals, and a sprinkle of fresh parsley makes any savoury dish look good.

Sage aids the digestion of rich, heavy fresh green foods, hence sage and onion stuffing for roast poultry is good kitchen medicine.

Summer savory Try a few leaves of this peppery herb in dishes containing beans and pulses – it will make them more digestible and improve their taste.

Tarragon A favourite herb of the French, fresh tarragon can be stuffed inside roast chicken, used to flavour wine vinegar, and added to omelettes and sauces. Always use fresh tarragon.

Thyme has a robust, aromatic flavour that enriches stews and soups made with beef or game. Use it also in marinades for meat or fish.

INDEX